LAUREN CONRAD
Beauty

ALSO BY LAUREN CONRAD

L.A. Candy

Sweet Little Lies
AN L.A. CANDY NOVEL

Sugar and Spice
AN L.A. CANDY NOVEL

Lauren Conrad Style

The Fame Game

Starstruck
A FAME GAME NOVEL

LAUREN CONRAD

Beauty

LAUREN CONRAD
WITH ELISE LOEHNEN

HARPER

An Imprint of HarperCollinsPublishers

Library of Congress Cataloging-in-Publication Data is available.

ISBN 978-0-06-212845-4

15 16 17 18 CG/RRDC 20 19 18 17 16 15 14 13 12

❖

First Edition

To my mother, who taught me that
being a beautiful person goes beyond hair
and makeup . . . but never failed to
remind me to get my roots done. I love you.

CONTENTS

INTRODUCTION ix

PREP

PLAY

INTRODUCTION

beauty |ˈbyü-tē|

noun (pl. **-ties**)

1: the quality or aggregate of qualities in a person or thing that gives pleasure to the
   senses or pleasurably exalts the mind or spirit : loveliness
2: a beautiful person or thing; *especially* : a beautiful woman
3: a particularly graceful, ornamental, or excellent quality
4: a brilliant, extreme, or egregious example or instance <that mistake was a *beauty*>
   —*Merriam-Webster Dictionary*

When I was a little girl, the first person I ever really thought of as beautiful was my own mother. She was, and still is, one of the most beautiful women I know: blond, beachy, effortlessly lovely. I remember watching from her bathroom floor as she sat at her vanity carefully applying makeup and loosely curling her hair. When it was time for her to get ready for a night out—whether it was date night with my father or a dinner party at a friend's house—she always knew how to apply her makeup just so. I was too young at the time to wear any makeup myself, but occasionally she would gift me an underused tube of lipstick or a compact of velvety pink blush. This was the '80s, when makeup smelled and tasted like *makeup*: powdery, old-fashioned, delicious. I still keep a few treasured old tubes of lipstick in my bathroom drawer. A hint of their thick scent and I am back on my mother's bathroom counter, palm pressed up against the mirror as I unevenly apply loud shades of red to my tiny lips and smear pale pink powder across my full cheeks. And then, I was beautiful too.

Just as she would sit back and let me dress myself in neon bike shorts, glitter-adorned T-shirts, and heart-shaped sunglasses, my mother let me define my own idea of beauty. When the time came for me to learn how to apply makeup in a less playful and more realistic fashion, my experience wasn't much different. In the seventh grade I was allowed to start wearing makeup, and to say this was a trial-and-error process is an understatement. I matched my eye shadows to my outfits each day, but took little care in matching my foundation to my actual skin tone. My eyebrows were overplucked and my hair overstraightened. I was a complete disaster. But that's what those awkward years are for, right? My mother never judged. (Luckily very few photos exist from this time in my life because most of them mysteriously disappeared . . . somehow.)

Aside from my mother, the other iconic blonde from my childhood was none other than Barbie. The long blond hair! The clothes! The impossibly tiny shoes! There was not one Barbie accessory that I did not clamor to own. I even had a My Size Barbie, which, at four feet tall, was, in retrospect, absolutely terrifying. From Barbie, I grew to embrace numerous Disney heroines: Cinderella, Snow White, Ariel, Belle, Jasmine. They may be unrealistic too, but at least I was being exposed to paradigms of beauty outside the Orange County norm. After all, I grew up in the land where bleached-out locks and bronzed skin reigned supreme.

When we're little, it is often the glittery trappings of beauty that we're most attracted to: Cinderella's shimmering ball gown; the crest of pale blue shadow that arcs across Barbie's almond eyes; Ariel's bejeweled bustier; Jasmine's impossibly long, silky raven hair. It's intoxicating. My attraction to these characters felt almost instinctual.

As we mature, so do our ideas of what's beautiful. I remember back in school, when a particular girl would be deemed most dateable and a certain boy would be deemed most kissable. The spotlight would shine brightly on those who were collectively—and arbitrarily—named Best in Show, and everyone else would just kind of blend into the background. The rest of us were dateable and kissable, sure, but not the prized possessions. That sort of communal brainwashing lessens in time as we all figure out what's attractive to *us*. As we define our own beautiful.

Even though I've grown up, changed, and grown up some more, I will still always feel that my mother is the most beautiful woman around. And if there's one thing my mother taught me that I can pass along to you it's that less is more when it comes to finding your look. When I moved out of Orange County, my hair grew darker, my tan faded, I stopped abusing eyeliner (for the most part), and I started to admire boys who didn't captain the water-polo team. I began experimenting more with my style, with hair and makeup—and learned a lot about myself and what looks good on me, in the process. One of the best parts of growing up is finding the freedom to model yourself on what feels most true (and is generally most flattering), rather than reflect what's around you. (Read: My overtreated, overlightened hair color wasn't doing anything for me, even though it was the shade of choice of nearly all my girlfriends.)

Fortunately for me, when I accidentally and unexpectedly stumbled into the entertainment industry, it came with one big perk: a beauty team. I would spend hours prior to each photo shoot and appearance in a cloud of hair spray and translucent powder only to emerge a new and improved me. Over the years I've worked with many talented makeup artists and hairstylists and have learned a lot from them. Every session in the chair is like a beauty 101 class. I study their techniques and ask about their choice products, and each time I learn something new. I will probably never be able to accomplish the same results as they do, but after years of practice I've gotten pretty decent at doing my own hair, makeup, and nails. This book is an opportunity for me to share with you everything I've learned along the way.

While working on this project I really began to think about the intangible idea of beauty, which truly is fascinating. And here's the conclusion I came to: While I hope you find the how-tos and lists helpful, I don't want you to follow the advice thinking you should look like me—that's why my face isn't the only one in this book. I've learned what beauty means to me and how to look and feel like the best version of myself, but I have also rejoiced in the fact that we don't all look the same. I hope you discover this too and that you use the information in this book to look and feel like your best version of you.

CHAPTER ONE
Finding Your Beauty

When *Teen Vogue* offered me an internship back in 2007, I was thrilled. I couldn't wait to begin working for the magazine I had idolized forever. But before I was allowed to fetch soy lattes and make color copies, they did have one request: that I immediately go to have my hair fixed. They even made me an appointment at Neil George Salon and requested the colorist "de–Orange County" my overprocessed locks. A little awkward and embarrassing, but ultimately it was a blessing: To this day, I'm so grateful for *Teen Vogue* and their West Coast editor Lisa Love's beauty intervention. My hair was horribly damaged from a combination of bleach and sun, and it was much too blond for my skin tone. In my defense, it had never even occurred to me that I should, or even could, deviate from the Laguna Beach norm. I had gone to the same hairdresser for the majority of my life and submitted my scalp to the same treatment as my friends. I was simply a reflection of an Orange County standard of beauty. As we grow up, we're "taught" what beauty is by what we see around us. It was pretty easy for me to blend in—my skin tanned easily, and I was born with naturally blond hair. But I can't imagine how difficult this must have been for the girls I grew up with who didn't fit the mold: It can be downright terrifying to wander through high school feeling different.

Not that I hadn't done my fair share of experimenting with beauty, occasionally ending in some comic moments: When I was in the fifth grade, I glued a rhinestone *bindi* to my forehead in an effort to look like Gwen Stefani. Not only was it not Halloween, but I used skin-bonding glue. I found it while rummaging through my mother's desk drawer and misinterpreted "skin bonding" as a purpose rather than a warning. It was exactly what I needed . . . to look completely stupid. (I still don't recall how I got it off.) And as for hair, I'd had the same long, blond hairstyle since I was young, so when eighth grade rolled around I knew it was time for a change . . . and when I saw a poster for the *Josie and the Pussycats* movie, I knew just what I wanted to do. I chopped my long hair to an inch above my shoulders and styled it with mousse to flare out (see page 12). When I decided to take it one step further and experiment with color, my first experience was similar to most girls': out of a box and done over my bathroom sink. The dark maroon I had selected was slightly rebellious but really wouldn't have been *that* bad, except that it was the exact same shade as the soccer uniform I was handed the next day at school. Enter: my hat phase. But until I moved to Los Angeles and started to develop my own aesthetic, I was pretty lost.

All of my friends' beauty journeys are similarly lined with horrible hair moments (of the dye, volume, and length variety), unfortunate makeup choices (brown lip liner, visible contouring, roll-on glitter), and bad signs of the times (overstraightening, gel, butterfly clips). It's all just part of growing up and figuring out who you are.

When I left that Lisa Love–approved salon back in 2007, I looked infinitely better. My damaged ends had been trimmed, and my shade resembled one that actually could have grown from my own head. It was the first time I'd been to a hairstylist who could telegraph what would work best with my face shape and coloring. (To be fair to my past hairstylist, I *had* requested the prior shade.) I ended up looking more like myself, and I liked it. I now had a solid foundation for my look: I began toning down my makeup as well and learned how to work *with* my features, rather than despite them.

Even though I rarely stray from my basic look these days (which is why shooting the images for chapter 12 was so much fun!), I still experiment regularly, and I still try my own version of many beauty trends, because there's always the promise that I might find a new technique or product that delivers everything I didn't know I needed. But in general I stick with subtle variations on a central theme. And that's what the first part of this book is about—finding your starting point, the essence of your basic look that you can return to again and again. Because playing dress-up is fun and can be helpful in evolving your style, but it's also good to look in the mirror and recognize what you see.

One Simple Thing You Can Do Every Day

Give yourself a compliment every day. I know this sounds silly, but it really is important. As girls, we spend countless hours focusing on our flaws and trying to correct them or cover them up. It's essential to focus on something you like about yourself. Maybe you're having a good hair day or your skin is looking especially healthy. Take a moment each day to focus on the good, and then try to carry that with you throughout the day, because while bangs don't look good on everyone, confidence does.

FAMOUS BEAUTIES

Unless you have an identical twin, you get to own your own beauty, but that doesn't mean that it's not incredibly helpful to use women you think are beautiful as inspiration while you're on the road to defining your own sensibility. If you'd like to subscribe wholesale to someone's aesthetic, it probably goes without saying that it's helpful to choose a role model you have things in common with. Unless you share features, face shape, coloring, or hair texture, it won't be quite as effective to try channeling someone who shares none of your attributes. If you're just looking for general tricks (how Jennifer Aniston colors her hair or how J. Lo achieves that perfect glow), then pull inspiration shots from far and wide. I tend to like the classic beauties, such as Audrey Hepburn, Brigitte Bardot, Catherine Deneuve, Sophia Loren, Natalie Wood, and Grace Kelly, but I have some contemporary favorites as well, including Michelle Williams, Charlize Theron, Zoe Saldana, Camilla Belle, Freida Pinto, and Kate Bosworth.

On the Subject of Celebrities . . .

The invention of high-definition TV was quickly followed by HD-friendly makeup. That, my friends, is because the veneer of perfection that you see painted across the small screen, the silver screen, billboards, and the glossy pages of magazines is often far from the truth (with the exception of cruel tabloids). We're all spackled, whether to combat breakouts, disproportionate features, dark circles, wrinkles, or the million and one other issues we could complain about. We're tuned-up by the industry's best hair and makeup artists, who can give us perfect bow-shaped lips; the sort of contouring that instantly makes us look ten pounds lighter; and beautiful, windblown waves. Then, because even that's not enough, a master retoucher will take a magnifying glass to the final image and meticulously correct every errant hair, wrinkle, or blemish with the powers of Photoshop or, in the case of television, really soft, hazy lenses. Photoshop has become such a necessity in the entertainment industry today that the leaking of an unretouched image onto the internet is cause for a scandal. In this book, and in *Lauren Conrad Style*, while of course there is some airbrushing, I've made sure it doesn't go overboard, because I feel very strongly that the image I project should be what I actually am—a fairly normal girl, with fairly normal problems. (I'll get into those later, I promise.)

I guess what I'm trying to say here is that we're all—*all*—surrounded by absolutely unrealistic ideas of beauty, because those girls in the photos, well, they're not *real*. They are the result of a hairstylist, a makeup artist, a manicurist, a personal stylist, a tailor, good lighting, correct angles, retouching. . . . And to get that one photo that makes the cut, sometimes a thousand or more need to be taken. So look at them for artistic inspiration only—for cool eye-shadow color combos, for blush placement, for unexpected ways to wear your hair—but please don't think for a second that you should look like them. Because nobody does—not even them.

You know those magnifying mirrors that can usually be found in hotel bathrooms? Those horrible, internally lit inventions that illuminate every pore, every wisp of hair above your upper lip, every incoming blemish (aka my sworn enemy)? Well, it's taken me years of finding the power of self-restraint, but I finally learned to resist the urge to flip the light switch and destroy my face, particularly in advance of an important photo shoot or appearance. We'll touch on blemishes later in the book, but a good, general rule is that only an excellent aesthetician should ever be armed with something that magnifies imperfections: Not only is it disconcerting to see a blackhead that's otherwise indiscernible to the eye, but it can be very damaging to put your hands all over your face.

MY BEAUTY EVOLUTION
(HINT: IT WASN'T ALWAYS PRETTY)

That's right. It's a Glamour Shot! I was thirteen years old, and it was the first time I'd ever had my hair and makeup done professionally.

I based this haircut off a *Josie and the Pussycats* poster. What was I thinking?

The eye shadow and mismatched foundation I wore to my winter formal junior year still haunts me to this day.

This bleached and straightened hair wasn't doing me any favors. My *Teen Vogue* beauty intervention came just in time!

This was the first time I ever wore liquid eyeliner. From that point on I couldn't go without it.

I wanted to downplay the elegance of the gown I wore this day with a chic ponytail and simple makeup.

By the time I celebrated my twenty-fifth birthday, I had my look down. No beauty team required here.

Nowadays I prefer my hair a more natural color and my makeup subtle.

CHAPTER TWO

Skin Care

When I was growing up, I would see those face-wash commercials and find them to be a little confusing, because the girls they featured were already so fresh-faced and pretty—they didn't seem to need the products! I understood the concept—*use our face washes and you'll be pretty too*—but I knew there must be a catch. And there is: Your skin can be completely unpredictable. I know mine has been for the past decade. I've definitely faced my share of breakouts, and at some of the most inopportune times. (Thank you, skin, for the surprise in the center of my forehead one day before that blind date.) And acne isn't the only skin issue I've had to deal with over the years. I have a persistent case of Melasma (skin discoloration around my forehead, eyes, and upper lip), unsightly eczema (when I touch salt water, sand, or even sushi, my hands literally peel), and stubborn Keratosis pilaris (that rashlike situation that might be on your upper arms and is only treatable with prescription creams and lasers). So if there's not a pre–red carpet blemish that I'm trying to outmaneuver, there's generally always something else. Side bangs can usually cover a forehead breakout, I opt for sleeves or body makeup when my Keratosis pilaris is acting up, and layers of heavy-duty concealer can usually camouflage my Melasma. The point is most of us are battling one form of flawed skin or another, so it is important to learn the difference between the things that are out of our hands and the things we can prevent.

While hormones and other mysterious skin reactions are often beyond our control, there is one damage-inducing factor that you can combat: the sun. Growing up in the almost-always-sunny climate of Southern California, I thought that the sun was my friend. Between three-hour-long tennis practices and afternoons spent at the beach, I baked in the sun on a regular basis. I never thought to wear sunscreen because I have an olive complexion and rarely burned. I had no idea the irreparable damage I was doing to my skin. When we're young, our skin is particularly prone to long-lasting damage—it's like a soft, vulnerable sponge—which is how I found myself in my dermatologist's office at the age of *fourteen* getting precancerous cells cut off my back (and yes, it left scars). For the rest of my life, I will visit my dermatologist at least twice a year for full-body checks because of the very high probability that there will be more early indications of skin cancer to come.

These days I don't leave the house without applying a healthy dollop of sunscreen. And while I love spending an afternoon at the beach, I tend to do so with a wide-brimmed hat, a cover-up . . . and a giant umbrella. Even with these precautions, I'll never be out of the woods. Take it from me: Wear your sunscreen, don't try to change your skin tone by three Pantone shades, and hopefully you'll never have to have the sun's effects scalpelled off your skin. Besides, there's really no need: Self-tanners these days are so believable, it's hard to justify tanning the old-fashioned way.

FINDING THE RIGHT SKIN-CARE REGIMEN FOR YOU— AND STICKING WITH IT

The basic condition of your skin has a lot to do with genes (feel free to blame your parents if you're not happy with yours—this one truly is their fault), but it's you who's responsible for its general upkeep, so don't slack. Not to state the obvious, but we all have wildly different skin; we even have different skin on different parts of our faces. Likely, you're some combination of oily, dry, and normal; you might even be excessively dry or excessively oily—and this can all change from day to day and week to week, depending on the weather, what's happening in your life, your hormonal cycle, or so many other factors. So, finding just one product that's going to answer all of your problems can be difficult, as much as skin-care companies would like us to believe that it's easy to classify and categorize all of us. If you've ever gone to see a facialist and watched her prescribe products, you'll note how varied the array will be. Unless she has her own product line, each item will likely be from a different source and theoretically for different types of skin. To find your ideal mix, start doing your research: Ask your dermatologist, poll any aesthetician you come in contact with, and use the internet as the library of information it is (but make sure your sources are reliable). I've learned just as much information from online forums about my Melasma—from people who suffer from the same thing—as I have from some of the most sought-after pros in Los Angeles.

What you will hear from people you should listen to is that you must give a new regimen time to work. The path to clear skin is not an overnight hike. It's a journey. Our skin works in cycles; every few weeks the skin cells regenerate (which is part of why it can take a blemish so long to fade), so you should plan to give your skin at least one cycle, and possibly two, to adjust to a new set of products and begin to react favorably. Think of it like a healthy diet and exercise plan: It can take a couple of weeks for your body to acknowledge that it's time to kick it into gear, at which point it begins to show improvement. The other thing to keep in mind: If a product sounds too good to be true, it likely is.

Once you find a product combination that works, stick with it! It's a common misconception that once you've "cured" your acne, rosacea, or eczema, it's gone for good. Not so! You must continue to maintain your routine if you'd like to maintain the results. Don't backslide after you've put in so much hard work!

Even if you're diligent about your skin-care regimen and diet, between makeup and pollutants in the air, toxins will inevitably find their way into your skin and will need to be extracted. That's why I firmly believe that everyone should have a good aesthetician (aka a facialist), who can provide the occasional deep cleansing and guidance on product choice. It doesn't have to happen every month or even every other month—a couple times a year is enough depending on the condition of your skin.

Basic Skin-Care Advice

Once you've picked a set of products to try—and committed to sticking with them for at least a month—you can use these basic at-home skin-care rules that I've learned from my years of grilling aestheticians. This is generally what keeps my skin in good shape.

CLEANSING

We all know that girl with the milk-and-honey complexion who never washes her face. That might work for her, but for the rest of us, getting our skin clean—in the morning and at night—is essential. You need to get the debris out of your pores so that they can breathe and also so that every product you apply—whether to treat acne or supply hydration—can be absorbed. Be warned though that you cannot "wash" acne away. In fact, if you clean your skin too aggressively, you can not only exacerbate it and cause inflammation, but you can trigger your oil glands to increase their production. It's a good idea to follow basic cleansing with some (alcohol-free) toner, especially if your skin is oily. Witch hazel can be a good, natural alternative to toner.

If you don't wear a lot of makeup, then using your hands to cleanse should be adequate. Get your hair out of your face and off your neck, and then in a circular motion work your cleanser into a lather across all zones of your face. Spend equal time on your cheeks and your chin (they're often overlooked in favor of the forehead), and make sure to get below your chin, your upper neck, and behind your ears and along your hairline, where residue can build up (particularly from hair products). This process should take at least a full minute—don't just lather up, rub your cheeks, and think you're done. Be sure to rinse well—you don't want to leave any cleanser on your face.

If you wear a lot of makeup, you might need extra help, from either an exfoliating cloth (keep a few on hand so you can throw them in the wash after each use), a Clarisonic face brush, or makeup remover and a cotton ball. If you go with makeup remover, use it before you wash your face, so that you can also clean off any residue it leaves behind. Another alternative is to wash your face twice.

EXFOLIATING

If you rub your fingertips across your face—particularly around its perimeter—and you feel a bit of roughness, this is likely due to clogged pores. Dead skin cells, dirt, oil, and makeup can get stuck in your pores and cause blemishes. You want to prevent this buildup so that the skin underneath can breathe. Whenever I feel a bit of roughness, which is usually once or twice a week, I use an exfoliator on my face. If your skin is sensitive, you'll still need to exfoliate, but to be extra-gentle, dilute your exfoliant by mixing it in with your cleanser. If your skin looks red or raw, *do not* exfoliate. If you have acne, look for an exfoliating cleanser that has a small amount of salicylic or glycolic acid in it.

MOISTURIZING

Even if you have oily skin, you'll still want to use a light, oil-free moisturizer across all zones of your face and your neck. And to ensure that you trap as much moisture as possible, it's most effective to apply hydrating creams to subtly damp skin. If you tend to have drier, flakier skin, exfoliate then slather on a cream immediately. Moisturizing is essential in the winter, especially if you live in a cold climate.

WHEN TO SEEK A DOCTOR'S OPINION

Since there's not that much you can do to treat serious skin issues from the outside in, if you have problematic skin—cystic acne, painful eczema, etc.—you should absolutely see a dermatologist. Don't pick at your face or read an article and think you're an expert. Your doctor will know what's going on and will work with you to find the right combination of products (some of which might be available by prescription only) to help you get your skin under control.

Lesson Learned

Not to call into question everything in this chapter, but no matter how well you wash your face and moisturize, if you don't get some rest, your skin is going to suffer. I used to think I could stay out late the night before a photo shoot or event, but it's just not true. Now when I have to be on set, I am usually tucked into bed by eleven the night before. There's a reason people call it "beauty sleep."

INGREDIENTS TO AVOID

Rather than tell you what products to buy (which I don't want to do, because the best products and brands are constantly changing), I want to provide you with a list of ingredients to try to avoid. While I've been told that even products that are best at penetrating the outer layers of skin can't reach the bloodstream, I still try to buy products with ingredient lists that are as natural (and short) as possible. One good indicator that a product isn't good for you? A lengthy string of words that you can't pronounce. Keep in mind that all things that sound terrible aren't necessarily bad. After all, even water is a chemical (H_2O). Also know that just because something proclaims that it's "natural" or "green" or "organic" doesn't mean that it's healthy—the FDA has been notoriously lax in laying out guidelines for what these words mean. Often it's a completely false claim. And sometimes things that are natural aren't necessarily good: Arsenic? Natural.

Below are some ingredients I try my best to avoid, but be aware that this list is by no means comprehensive. You can find a lot of information about toxic chemicals on www.fda.gov/cosmetics, via www.safecosmetics.org, and also through www.ewg.org/skindeep/ (the Skin Deep database at Environmental Working Group), where you can look up products to determine what harmful ingredients they might contain. (It's a little alarming how many things we're told to avoid—try not to freak yourself out. But the information is constantly updated, so keep it bookmarked.)

FRAGRANCE
When it comes to skin care, I try to skip anything that contains synthetic fragrance, which studies show might be carcinogenic. While I want my hair to smell good, I don't need my face to (unless it comes from naturally yummy ingredients, like rose hips or bergamot).

PHTHALATES
These commonly go by dibutyl phthalate (DBP), dimethyl phthalate (DMP), and diethyl

phthalate (DEP) and can be found in some skin products, hair sprays, and nail polish. (They're plasticizers, so they make nail polish and hair spray less brittle.) They're constantly on the FDA's watch list, and while not proven to be harmful in low doses, I try to avoid them when possible. Studies suggest that phthalates are hormone-disrupting and are one of the reasons that girls hit puberty so young these days. (They're also one of the reasons that pregnant women are sometimes advised not to use nail polish . . . seems like warning enough to me!)

DIETHANOLAMINE

This is used in cosmetics to create a foaming effect. While the FDA states that it's safe in low doses, I try to skip cosmetics that contain DEA or DEA-related ingredients, which include: Cocamide DEA, Cocamide MEA, DEA-Cetyl Phosphate, DEA-Oleth-3 Phosphate, Lauramide DEA, Linoleamide MEA, Myristamide DEA, Oleamide DEA, Stearamide MEA, TEA-Lauryl Sulfate, and Triethanolamine.

COAL-TAR COLORS & DYES

These have been proven to be carcinogenic, and many are banned. Those that are still in use pass safety tests and are marked as either FD&C or D&C. If the former, that means the color is safe to be consumed (and is, accordingly, safe for your skin). If it's D&C or Ext D&C, it's only safe for topical application. According to general guidelines, do not apply any product labeled Ext D&C near your eyes or on your lips.

FORMALDEHYDE

I used to think only undertakers used this. Not so. Formaldehyde is frequently used in beauty products because it's an antibacterial and a preservative. But it's a known carcinogen so avoid it when possible. Some ingredients in mascara break down and become formaldehyde, which is why you should replace your mascara every few months.

ALUMINUM

A common ingredient in antiperspirant, since it plugs sweat ducts (which is kind of gross anyway), aluminum has been known to be absorbed by the skin and behave like estrogen (which means it can foster cancer-cell growth).

PARABENS

Parabens (often preceded by methyl-, ethyl-, butyl-, or propyl-) are preservatives designed to make products last longer (instead of something natural, like vitamin E, which isn't as effective over the long term). Parabens interfere with hormones and can be absorbed through the skin. They are a big deal in terms of ingredients to avoid, so these days it's pretty easy to find products that are paraben-free.

ACNE

High school is hard enough—why does acne have to make it unbearable some days? Oh, and whoever said acne goes away after high school is a liar. So, whether you're fifteen, thirty-five, or somewhere in between, you will probably be dealing with blemishes.

BLACKHEADS

Up until my early twenties, I always assumed that a blackhead indicated that your face was, well, dirty. That's not exactly true. A blackhead forms when your pores get clogged. When the clogged oil (otherwise known as sebum, which even sounds gross) interacts with the air, it turns black. While you can squeeze blackheads out, they'll keep coming back. If they're problematic (we all have some, and they're usually not very visible), see a dermatologist, who will likely prescribe some sort of gel or scrub to really clean out the pores, or see a facialist to get extractions.

WHITEHEADS

Despite the fact that these are under the skin and therefore not exposed to oxygen (which is why they're white), whiteheads are often more noticeable than blackheads—especially to you. (Sometimes it's hard to remember that no one is scrutinizing your face as closely as you are.) But even though you might have one that looks ready for popping, resist the urge. Letting it run its course will help you avoid giving yourself a scar. If you have an especially troubling whitehead and just can't let it lie, one thing you can do is dab at the blemish with an ice cube covered in a paper towel or cloth. The ice takes down inflammation and redness and kills bacteria, and you can safely do this several times a day. After only a few times, it should be in better shape to be covered.

How to Pop a Zit

The short answer to this is: don't, particularly if you have scar-prone skin. Not only can you damage the skin around the pimple, but you can also inflame it and increase its duration. If you squeeze, you can also cause the head to burst inward (which can spread the bacteria under the surface of the skin and cause more breakouts). If you have a very painful red cyst or nodule, do not touch it. Contact your dermatologist for a cortisone injection, which can make the swelling subside.

If you absolutely must tackle it, and you're convinced that it's ready, wash your face really well and place a hot washcloth on the zit to draw it out as much as possible (or start your procedure immediately post-shower). Wrap each of your index fingers with facial tissue and apply a small amount of pressure a few millimeters away from the edge of the zit. (Again, don't press down directly on top of it.) If it doesn't "pop" right away, leave it alone. If it does "pop," make sure it pops fully. Cleanse your face again and apply a little toner (or witch hazel).

BODY ACNE

There's nothing more frustrating than body acne, which is incredibly prevalent. Think about it: Your back is covered with oil-producing pores that are generally covered with layers of fabric. It's no wonder they're inclined to get clogged. But it's fairly easy to combat if you clean your back properly by using a plastic-bristle brush (the plastic won't breed bacteria like a "natural"-bristle brush) to scrub it with soap. You can also treat bacne with a topical benzoyl peroxide. (Be careful though! Benzoyl peroxide can bleach any fabric it touches, so don't wear fancy pj's or sleep on your favorite sheets right after you put it on.) Chest acne is a bit trickier, since the skin across your clavicle is delicate. You can wash the area gently with a shower puff. Breakouts here are highly hormonal and will usually fade without treatment. Do your best to keep your hands off of it.

READING YOUR FACE

Recently I've become a bit obsessed with aestheticians who have a deep understanding of Eastern medicine and face mapping. The idea is that there's a strong correlation between your internal organs—and other things happening in your body—and different zones of the face. For example, issues with your liver will show up as redness in the center of your forehead. A breakout here might signify overly rich foods in your diet or an allergy to dairy. One aesthetician I see regularly can tell which side I ovulated on that month by examining my chin under her magnifying glass—and she can sense when I've just been sick or am about to get sick based on the areas directly above my eyebrows. It can be a really fun and interesting way to find out what might be happening internally—it makes sense too, if you keep in mind that your skin is actually an organ. Here is a basic face map showing some of the areas where breakouts occur and their common causes.

1 FOREHEAD: Breakouts across the forehead can be triggered by stress or sleep deprivation.

2 ABOVE BROW: The area above the brows represents your immune system. Breakouts tend to appear before, after, or during a cold or flu.

3 BETWEEN BROWS: Breakouts between the brows are often caused by overindulgence. Try cutting back on sugar, rich foods, and alcohol.

4 CHEEKS: Your cheeks are affected by your lung quality. Smoking or breathing polluted air can cause breakouts here.

5 SIDE OF CHIN: The sides of your chin are affected by hormones. Breakouts occur around the time of your period and more on one side depending on which ovary is ovulating that month.

THE WORST THINGS FOR YOUR SKIN

Sun

Contrary to popular belief, baking in the sun doesn't clear up acne, especially if it's acne on your face. It might modify your skin tone so that your blemishes aren't as visible, and it might dry up the outer layer of skin, but it can actually exacerbate the problem, particularly if you're prone to rosacea or on a medication that's light-sensitive (like Retin-A).

And speaking of sun, don't forget to apply SPF on your chest, neck, and hands, as the thinner layers of skin there are the first to show sunspots. You can do everything to maintain a young-looking face and quickly give yourself away elsewhere. There are great natural and mineral-based sunscreens on the market that don't contain scary chemicals—a small powder formulation with a brush attached is something I always keep in my purse too, in case I need to apply extra sunscreen on the go. (It's invisible.) And because it's not a liquid, it's excellent for traveling. You don't need to pull out the SPF 45 on a daily basis—and you shouldn't avoid the sun completely, since that could end in you having a vitamin-D deficiency. Anything in the SPF 15 to 30 range should be enough for everyday protection.

I said it before and I'll say it again: If you've been exposed to too much sun throughout your life, be sure to submit yourself to a full-body check by your dermatologist. Skin cancer can be fatal; it's key to catch it early. And if you're obsessed with having bronzed skin, and makeup doesn't cut it, look into sunless tanners. There are countless options on the market that deliver a natural glow.

SMOKING

In addition to all the horrible things smoking can do to your health, it's another way to destroy your face. Not only because you'll get wrinkles around your mouth, but because smoking speeds up the aging process of the skin. It's a gross habit, so just try to steer clear of it.

DEHYDRATION

Your skin is your body's largest organ and it needs hydration to function at its best. Drink plenty of water and your skin cells will be plump and healthy.

PICKING AT YOUR FACE

This one's easy—picking at your face will only exacerbate whatever's going on there. Hands off for a happier complexion. And make sure to keep your phones and glasses clean because they can harbor bacteria that you don't want touching your face.

One Simple Thing You Can Do Every Day

I know I've pretty much hit you over the head with the SPF message, but there's one more thing you need to hear: Your lips need protection from the sun too. Add a lip balm with sunscreen to your collection, and you're covered. There are tinted ones, so you can be protecting your mouth and prettying up at the same time. Look for a natural one, so you can be sure you're not eating chemicals when you lick your lips.

CHAPTER THREE

Hair Care

While I've always been pretty conservative when it comes to experimenting with my makeup, I've taken many more chances with my hair. I've worn it red, brown, blond, pink, blue, straight, curly, long, short . . . And while I inevitably return to my dirty-blond locks each time, I've enjoyed my brief affairs with change. I think of my hair as an accessory with the potential to elevate any look. If I'm heading out for a fun dinner with friends adorned in sequins, I might give my hair volume and curls. If I'm attending a charity brunch, it might be polished and garnished with a bow. There is so much fun to be had with your hair, and when it comes to styling, it's all temporary. You're just one wash and blow-dry away from your tried-and-true style. So have fun with it.

But before the fun can start, it's best to learn a little about what hair actually is and how to make sure you're taking good care of yours. Hair covers every square inch of our bodies—except for the palms of our hands, the soles of our feet, and our lips—although in some places it's barely perceptible. And strands of hair are actually composed of "dead" cells, which is funny when you realize we've been instructed throughout our lives to keep our hair healthy. The only part that is "alive" is the follicle—the bulb implanted in the scalp—which you can see if you accidentally tug out a strand of hair. The follicle is responsible for producing oil, for generating the melanin that gives our hair its color (if you go gray, that's because your follicle is not creating your color anymore), and for flexing to create goose bumps.

For the most part, your hair is what it is. Sure, you can straighten it, perm it, color it, or beat it into general submission, but that head of hair is yours for a reason. It's something you've inherited. And just as it can be futile to rail against the shape of your body, your hair probably looks best when it's closest to its natural color and texture. Which is not to say that you can't maximize on all of its great qualities with the right cut and styling techniques. This chapter is all about proper hair care—plus I'll give you some guidelines for knowing what to ask for at the salon to ensure that you're left with as few bad-hair days as possible.

DAILY HAIR CARE

Since your hair is actually dead, you can't do much to improve it on a cellular level—but you *can* damage and destroy it, so it's important to take proper care of it every day.

How Frequently You Should Wash Your Hair

Some professionals say you should only lather up once a week, while others swear this is something that needs to be done on a daily basis. My hairstylist, Kristin Ess, is on the less-is-more side of this. The follicles in our scalps produce sebum (the oil that makes our hair greasy) at varying rates (more right before that time of the month). If you wash your hair every day, you strip that oil from the scalp, causing your follicles to produce sebum at a greater rate to compensate. You can change that, though, and coach your follicles to produce less oil, by gradually washing your hair less frequently (going from washing it every day to every other day, then to every third day, etc.). This is great news for those of us who like to style our hair, because the less often you do a full-on styling routine (i.e., blowing out your hair and curling it every morning), the healthier your hair will stay. If you have long hair, the night before you're planning to skip a wash, sleep with your hair in a loose braid (or two loose braids) to avoid waking up with serious bedhead.

For those times when you want to make your blowout last for an extra day, there's always dry shampoo, which is essentially a spray-on powder that absorbs excess oil. But use it sparingly—no more than a couple times a week. If you find that you're trying to extend time between shampoos with *too much* dry shampoo, then you should be washing your hair more often. It's important to not let sebum build up on your scalp. Like with your skin, the pores on your head can get blocked and clogged, which can lead to issues like hair loss. You don't want to overwash it, but you need to make sure that you're keeping it clean and healthy.

What's in a Shampoo?

Shampoo is a relatively new concept. Historically people used body soap to wash their hair (which, due to a lot of soap residue, made their strands dull and their scalps itch)—and they didn't do it that often. Around the early 1900s, chemists started experimenting with products, and soon after, shampoos hit the market. But it wasn't until the '70s that people started to lather up their heads with any real frequency.

These days, shopping the shampoo aisle can be downright perplexing: There are products for every complaint, from dandruff to frizziness. And they span a huge range of price points. While I believe that shampoos with more natural ingredients are worth some extra money, *Consumer Reports* did a much-quoted test (they used *seventeen hundred ponytails* in the study) and found that there was pretty much no difference at all between the top and the bottom of the shampoo market. So next time you're browsing the aisle remember that you really don't need to spend a small fortune on a bottle of shampoo.

Keep in mind that shampoo is for cleaning your scalp, not strands of hair, so focus the product on the roots. If you have oilier hair, choose a shampoo that is clear—those that are creamy or pearlescent generally contain more conditioners, which you do *not* need to apply to your scalp. Many grease-fighting varieties contain astringent ingredients that are helpful, like tea-tree or citrus oil or herbs like rosemary and sage.

If your scalp is flaky, you should look for a product that fights dandruff. The active ingredient in these is usually zinc pyrithione, which has antifungal properties. Other products actually slow the rate at which your cells die and need to be sloughed off.

If your scalp feels tight and itchy, look for a moisturizing shampoo that's packed with hydrating ingredients like shea butter and nut oils. This can also help combat flakiness.

WHAT'S IN A CONDITIONER?

Unlike shampoo, conditioners can change the quality of your hair, since they coat and adhere to the cuticle of the strand and lend it all sorts of properties. (Again, conditioners are not changing your hair's inherent properties—just modifying that outer layer.) Conditioners with lots of humectants deliver moisture; those with lots of panthenol attach to overly fine strands and create the illusion of volume; those with lots of polymers make hair look sleek and glossy and untangled; and those with heat-absorbing polymers help protect hair against curling irons, blow-dryers, and straighteners.

Because conditioners are packed with ingredients that are intended to attach to the strand, you don't want to apply conditioner to your scalp—instead deposit a majority of it on the bottom two-thirds of your hair, specifically the back of your head, where the hair is most directly exposed to harsh elements.

Every month or so, I like to wash my head with a clarifying shampoo to help strip some of the residue left by conditioners. Excessive buildup can eventually start to make my hair feel and look a little limp. I also always ask for a gloss or deep conditioning when I get my color done. It makes a difference in keeping my hair looking healthy longer.

While skin is an actual organ, hair is dead, so ingredients in conditioner are less likely to be absorbed. However, the shampoo on your scalp is a different story. If you need a refresher course in what to avoid in makeup and skin-care products (some of these bad guys, like DEA, often show up in hair products too), turn to page 24. For hair products I also look out for:

SODIUM LAURYL SULFATE AND SODIUM LAURETH SULFATE

Also known as SLS and SLES, these detergents are frequently found in shampoo. They're cheap to make and generate a lot of foam when lathered (which is expected in shampoo but not actually important for cleansing) but are a major skin irritant. There are studies about how they can damage the immune system and, when combined with other ingredients, become carcinogenic. The jury may be out, but I'm inclined to just avoid them.

TRIETHANOLAMINE (TEA)

Like DEA, this is a foaming agent. While it's not carcinogenic on its own, it can interact with other chemicals and become carcinogenic. Pass!

PROPYLENE GLYCOL

This is a humectant, which means it theoretically has moisturizing capabilities (it actually just makes hair a bit slippery), but it also shows up in antifreeze. It's thought to cause dermatitis, eczema, hives, and, what's worse, kidney, liver, and brain problems. No thanks!

Natural Hair Masks

I don't apply hair masks as often as face masks, but every month or so I like to mix up something in the kitchen, comb it through my hair, then wrap my head in a towel warm from the dryer or plastic wrap, which traps the natural heat your head emits (heat enhances the power of the mask—plus you have to protect your couch!), and watch a movie. Here are the recipes I use most often:

COCONUT OIL

Coat the ends of your hair with a tablespoon of coconut oil and then twist it into a low bun and seal it with plastic wrap. At a minimum, leave it for thirty minutes, but it's best if you can sleep with it in. Then shampoo and condition your hair as usual in the morning.

AVOCADO

Mash up an entire avocado and mix it with four tablespoons of yogurt and one egg white. You don't want this on your scalp either, just the bottom two-thirds of your hair. Leave on for at least thirty minutes. The egg and yogurt provide a major injection of protein for weakened hair while the avocado softens the strands. But make sure the water isn't too hot when you rinse it out or else the egg will get cooked and can stick in your hair. (Speaking from experience . . . it's gross.)

OLIVE OIL AND MAYONNAISE

This one is a bit tougher to stomach. Mix together a concoction that's equal parts mayo and olive oil (enough to give you a palmful of the finished product) to give dry and brittle hair a shot of moisture and antioxidants. Start at the ends and work up, stopping short of your scalp. After thirty minutes, wash it out with lukewarm water.

READER Q: HOW DO I GET MY HAIR TO GROW FASTER?

A vital part of getting your hair to grow faster is to protect the hair you already have. If your ends become damaged, you'll have to chop off a considerable number of inches to prevent the damage from extending up the shaft. (Once that end is split, it can travel right up the strand.) If you're trying to grow your hair out, it's more important than ever that you see your hairstylist for trims, as counterintuitive as that sounds. You can also do small things to speed up the growth rate marginally, but keep in mind that there are no miracles—don't shell out for products with claims that are completely unrealistic.

TO PROTECT THE HAIR YOU HAVE

- Work conditioner through your hair with a wide-tooth comb in the shower so that you're not trying to drag your brush through tangles after you get out.

- Minimize the amount of heat you use on your hair. And before you use a blow-dryer or a straightener, apply a serum to protect the strands. (It closes the cuticle and creates a barrier between the hair and the heat.) Never try to straighten or curl wet hair—the heat will steam out the water (and remove all the natural oils in your hair as well). In the long run, it can be very damaging.

- Don't pull your hair into overly tight ponytails. Not only can this pull your hair out, but it can damage your roots. There's a reason a too-tight ponytail starts to hurt after a while!

- Avoid sleeping with your hair in a ponytail secured with an elastic. Instead try a loose braid secured with . . . a scrunchie. (They have their uses in the privacy of your own home.)

To Promote Growth

- Eat well. Your follicles need a good mix of proteins and vitamins (A, C, E, B3, B6, and B12 are all key) to promote healthy growth. You also want to be sure that you're eating enough iron, which is found in tofu, lentils, beans, spinach, and lean beef.

- When you are shampooing or rinsing your hair with water, massage your scalp with your fingertips. This can increase blood circulation in the area and theoretically promotes growth.

- Avoid stress, which can cause hair to fall out. For more on stress and how it affects you, see chapter 4.

- Sometimes I take prenatal vitamins. They're not scientifically proven to make hair grow faster, but they have always worked for me (as well as terrified any guy I am dating).

One Simple Thing You Can Do Every Day

At some point—not that many years ago—my trusted hair guru, Kristin Ess, held up a mirror to the back of my hair to show a line of breakage that roughly coincided with where my hair tie hit when I threw my hair into a ponytail before a workout. Harsh elastics can take a serious toll on your hair and create that annoying little halo of frizzies. Since then, I only use elastic bands that don't have any metal fastenings and that are super-soft and nondamaging—like Twistbands (made from tie-dyed pieces of wide elastic).

FINDING THE RIGHT HAIRCUT

At some point we have all made that spontaneous decision to drastically alter our hairstyle. (This is known as a hair "breakover" because it often happens right after a breakup or other major life change.) Unfortunately, more often than not, this leaves us with regret followed by a lot of bad-hair days and ponytails. Now, when I'm considering making a drastic change to my hair, I start by trying on wigs that are similar to the cut and color I am contemplating. More than a few times this has steered me away from a poor hair decision (hello, bangs!). And today's technology can also help take some of the guesswork out of selecting a new cut—there are computer programs that allow you to try different hairstyles on a photo of yourself. (That's right—there's an app for that!) While these methods can be helpful in the decision-making process, no computer or hairpiece will ever be able to perfectly predict how your own hair's color and texture will interact with a particular haircut. So while it's not that hard to see how a cut will look in *theory* (either by uploading a photo onto one of these sites or heading to the wig shop to test-drive a 'do in person), it's impossible to know what you're actually going to end up with—and how you're going to maintain it.

We've all been drawn to a hairstyle or cut that we're convinced will be perfect but that our hair doesn't actually have the texture to support. When that happens you have to fall back on technique—and time—to get your hair into salon shape every morning, which can be a huge commitment. It's always great to bring pictures of styles you like to the salon, but be sure to be honest and open with your hairstylist about your ability to execute the upkeep on your own—and be flexible when your hairstylist guides you to a solution that might work better for your schedule and skill set!

To help you find your best look, here are some simple guidelines for different face shapes and hair textures. Keep in mind that these come from general consensus and basic principles (and a long chat with the brilliant Kristin Ess). Everyone is different, so listen to what your hairstylist is telling you will work for your unique face.

SQUARE

Your forehead and angular jawline are roughly the same width.

Play down your strong jawline with a longer length and soft waves. Don't cut bangs—they will draw the eye to your jaw. While you might feel compelled to use your hair as a curtain, it's better to open up your face. Wear your hair parted to one side, which will soften up your face's angles. If you want shorter hair, try a wavy bob so that it breaks up the lines of your face.

OVAL

Your forehead and jawline are a similar width, and your face is long.

Count yourself lucky because, if you have an oval face shape, you're pretty much safe no matter what style you choose: Almost anything will flatter. (My face is oval, although I definitely found some bad-hair directions for me—mostly of the cutting-my-own-bangs variety.) The key to finding the best cut is to look at your forehead. If it's shorter, like mine, you want to steer clear of bangs. If you have a longer forehead though, bangs are key, since they'll prevent your face from appearing too long.

ROUND

Your cheeks are full and wider than your jaw and forehead.

Because your face already has plenty of width, you will want to wear your hair as long as possible to narrow it out. (Layers will add unnecessary horizontal volume, so steer clear of anything too drastic.) You can also add a little volume at the top of your head (meaning, don't style your hair so it's plastered to your head—give it a little lift), since it will draw the eye up.

HEART-SHAPED

You have a wider forehead and cheekbones and a narrow jawline.

You definitely want to have some sort of soft, side-parted Reese Witherspoon–style bang. Don't cut them too blunt and straight, otherwise they'll make your chin look pointy. Go for a medium-long length with nice, choppy bangs. (Anything too long will pull down your chin.)

LONG AND NARROW

Your face is narrow from temple to chin and long.

To counteract the length, you want a long bob, or you can go longer if you have curly hair, in which case you should add some layers for a nice shape and volume. (The shortest layer should be just below your chin.) Bangs can work here too, since they will help break up the length of your face.

IF YOUR HAIR IS . . .

TYPE (STRAIGHT/WAVY OR CURLY/TIGHT CURLS): The natural state of your hair before any treatments or styling.

TEXTURE (COARSE/FINE): The thickness of the strands of hair. Coarse hair tends to be less shiny and harder to color. Fine hair can be too sensitive to color.

DENSITY (THIN/THICK): The amount of actual strands of hair on your head. The longer it takes your hair to dry naturally the thicker your density.

STRAIGHT + FINE + THIN: Add graduated layers to build up weight and volume. If you're speaking to your hairstylist, these are technically called convex layers.

A few years ago, before it ever occurred to me that I could try on a hairstyle at a wig shop before actually cutting my hair, I ended up with a blunt bob that looked less chic and more soccer mom. I was convinced that it would work with my hair texture, which is pretty thick and straight. Unfortunately, I was wrong. After about two days of sporting the short cut I called for the first available appointment to get hair extensions. Four years later it still hasn't returned to its original length.

STRAIGHT + FINE + THICK: Refer back to your face shape, since your hair is usually very manageable and whatever works best for your shape will work for your hair type. Layers are usually great, particularly if you want to add any volume up top.

STRAIGHT + COARSE + THIN: Graduated layers (i.e., convex layers) are best. A round brush can help you get your texture in check, but you will still want to add in some weight and volume.

STRAIGHT + COARSE + THICK: This is usually found in women with gray hair. You typically want to remove length around the face to avoid getting the dreaded frizzy triangle.

WAVY OR CURLY + FINE + THIN: Even though you have curls, you still want to add volume. (You don't want those curls to be flat and stuck to your head.) Ask for graduated layers.

WAVY OR CURLY + FINE + THICK: Your hair may be fine, but you have a lot of it, so you'll want to minimize the volume by adding layers to remove the "triangle" and cutting out some of the weight.

WAVY OR CURLY + COARSE + THIN: Before you make any moves here, consider how you wear your hair.

If you like to blow it out, give it some layers for movement. If you wear it curly, go with long layers around the face to keep it from looking bulky.

WAVY OR CURLY + COARSE + THICK: Layer it up! Taking out weight is key with this hair type. You'll want to remove the volume but keep the length.

TIGHT CURLS + COARSE: This is a very specific hair type and requires a specialized skill set, so be sure that the person cutting your hair knows what they're doing. Generally the hairstylist should cut your hair when it is dry, because if it's cut while wet it will shrink up afterward and become an entirely different shape. If your hair is short, add layers to build volume. If it's longer, layer it to remove weight and width.

TIGHT CURLS + FINE: Follow the same instructions as above, but go easy! Fine, tightly curled hair should be cut with caution because you can see the shape change so quickly.

READER Q: HOW MUCH HAIR LOSS IS NORMAL?

That mass of hair clogging the drain probably isn't cause for concern. We shed up to one hundred strands a day—but considering we have about one hundred thousand strands on our heads, it's not noticeable. If you're convinced that you're losing more than that, you should see a doctor (either your dermatologist or your general practitioner would be a good place to start). Excessive hair loss can be triggered by stress, anemia (a lack of iron, which is common in girls who have heavy periods), pregnancy, and age. Essentially anything that affects your hormones can send hair into the telogen phase, which is the period hair enters right before it falls out.

GENERAL GUIDELINES FOR COLORING YOUR HAIR

When you go darker, you'll find many color lines load their products with conditioning agents, so the layer of color can often make your hair feel soft and luxurious. Going lighter, however, can be fraught with issues. You need to take extra caution when caring for your hair, since you've inherently shifted it into more fragile territory. I've been way-too-blond in my life, and what's worse, I've gone too-blond too quickly. Resist the urge to shift your color more than one or two shades at a time. If you go too far, there's a good chance your hair might not look right, plus it will require constant—and expensive—upkeep. And then there's the irreversible damage.

Like with a haircut, it can be nearly impossible to determine exactly what the color is going to look like on your head, which is why, as tempting as the aisles of pretty hair-dye boxes may be, if you want to lighten your color, or go for a dramatic change, please go see a professional. Fixing a bad at-home job can take months—or, at worst, you will have to wait until your hair fully grows out (i.e., years). Before you sit down in the chair, tear out pictures of your favorite colors from magazines to bring to your stylist. And, again, go to a wig store and try on different shades to see how they interact with your skin tone. Listen to your colorist's recommendations so you don't end up with something too close to your own skin tone; it can make you appear monochromatic.

ALL ABOUT BANGS

Whether you've worn bangs or not, you probably realize that there's a lot of variety in the fringe family. If you're looking to really change up your look, but don't want to sacrifice length in either direction (that is, you're not about to chop it all off or add length with extensions), bangs can be a good solution. And this doesn't mean that you have to adopt dramatic, blunt bangs either. You can always trim more, so start with ones that are longer, and go from there.

LONG, SIDESWEPT BANGS

These are good for almost any hair type and can be very versatile. You can straighten them or wear them a bit wavy to blend them into curls. They're also easy to grow out, which makes them the perfect solution for easing yourself into a full-on bang commitment. These also work well if you have naturally curly hair that you let air-dry, since you can blow-dry the bangs and then sweep them to the side and blend them in with your other hair.

BLUNT EYEBROW-LENGTH BANGS

These are a good option if you have a long, narrow face, because they make your face appear a bit more oval. They're also great if you have thick, straight hair and want a more mod look. If your eyes are your favorite feature, these will draw a lot of attention to them!

51

How to Trim Your Own Bangs

It can be a pain to keep running to your hairstylist for bang trims, but most don't charge, so that should be your first option. If you absolutely can't see and are desperate, then proceed with caution.

First you should wash, dry, and straighten your bangs so that they make a clean, straight line. Then hold small sections of hair between two fingers and take eyebrow scissors (they're little) and hold them parallel to your hair. You're going to cut up at a slight angle—not across—in little, tiny snips. After you trim a few millimeters, take a step back from the mirror and assess before you cut any more.

WISPY-ENDED BANGS

You don't want your bangs to ever be too thin, otherwise they'll look a little '80s, but you can have your hairdresser cut up into an otherwise blunt bang just to make the ends more jagged and less precise. This is good if your hair has some body and you don't want your bangs to look too perfect.

CHAPTER FOUR

Stress

*B*ack in high school, before a big event like homecoming or prom, I would, like girls everywhere, inevitably suffer some sort of breakout. I always assumed that it was my body playing a cruel trick on me. It was clear that my body—not my mind—was in control. But as I learned more about how much stress can affect pretty much every area of your life, I realized that wasn't the case. There's a reason that the pimple-on-date-night cliché exists and follows us through the major events in our life, from school dances to weddings to job interviews: Stress messes with everything. It can agitate your skin, your hair, and your nails. It can even cause weight gain.

When I was filming *The Hills*, and managing the rest of my career, I felt completely overwhelmed: sleep-deprived, privacy-less (no surprise there!), and apprehensive, as all early-twenty-year-olds are, about my future. I wanted to succeed at everything—in the show, in my career in fashion, in my personal life. It was a lot to handle.

I finally went to see a doctor for advice, who cautioned me that stress not only poisons your body, it can actually be a form of addiction. While traditional "addicts" might use hard drugs as a release from stress, there's a whole different subset of people who don't know how to live without anxiety—for type A personalities, stress can be the pulse-quickening factor that drives them, at unhealthy speeds, through life. When you feel the signs of stress, what's actually happening is that your mind thinks you're in danger and is preparing you for it (the whole "flight or fight" response from our prehistoric days) by releasing more adrenaline and cortisol. This is great if you really are in danger and need to flee, but this is terrible for you when it happens on a regular basis. The constant uptick in these hormones wreaks havoc all over—your immune system suffers, skin problems can be exacerbated (the cortisol creates more oil, so your pores get clogged), you can become forgetful or depressed . . . For me, stress was taking a physical toll: My skin looked dull and blemished, I began to struggle to maintain my weight, and I even started to lose my hair. (In just one short year I lost much of my hair's body, both from fallout and from lackluster strands. Fortunately I had thick hair to begin with, and I was able to hide this loss with hair extensions and styling.) It was alarming, and considering I work in an industry where your appearance is under constant scrutiny, I knew I had to do something immediately.

So I took my doctor's advice and found ways to both relax and detox, and I made some major lifestyle changes. I began to educate myself on what I was putting into my body and how it was affecting me. I cut back on my caffeine intake (clearly my nervous system didn't need any more stimulation); I cut back on alcohol (it can impair sleep, and I needed my rest); I started eating better; I started exercising in a moderate way with more frequency. Sometimes spending an hour in the gym after a long day is the perfect way to de-stress. (Who needs therapy when you have kickboxing?) With some time and dedication, I finally got my anxiety levels back down to a very low simmer. Soon I looked and felt better: healthier, happier, glowing.

Since then I've worked hard to find balance in my life. Because, in order for me to do my job well, I need to look healthy and happy, and I won't look healthy and happy if I don't feel it. It's come down to a combination of good habits, figuring out the difference between what I can control (with ease) and what I need to let go, and pampering tricks and tips that help me calm down and relax immediately. I hope this chapter will lead you to ideas for finding balance too!

SLEEP DEPRIVATION

Isn't it ironic that when you were young your parents probably had to hog-tie you to your crib to get you to take a nap? What I wouldn't give for a mandatory two-hour siesta every afternoon. (Italy and Spain have the right idea . . . particularly because we're biologically set to feel a circadian dip in the afternoon, which is that sleepy, less-alert feeling.) I had to come to grips—far too early in life—that I would rarely see nine hours of sleep a night outside of a vacation. In high school I was getting to campus at the unseemly hour of 7:00 a.m. and staying up until the wee hours of the morning talking to my friends on the phone or, occasionally, pulling an all-nighter for an exam. In L.A. it's been late-night events, early-morning photo shoots, deadlines, traveling, and everything else in the leftover hours in between. And I'm expected to look camera ready, regardless of the toll the lack of sleep is taking on my under-eye circles! Thank goodness for concealer . . . and Photoshop.

Because I average about six to seven hours of sleep per night (a general baseline recommendation for teens is eight to ten hours and for adults is seven to nine hours of sleep, per the National Sleep Foundation), it is absolutely essential that those are quality hours. And that they're scheduled: I am very fortunate to have a fairly flexible schedule, since I happen to work best at night, when the incoming emails slow and my phone isn't ringing. This is when I get the bulk of my work done, whether it's research for my website, writing, or working on designs for one of my clothing lines. I love the quiet. Because of this, I've learned to avoid early meetings and appointments when scheduling my days. (My "just five more minutes" sixteen-year-old self would be so proud.) Everyone has different sleeping patterns. The most important thing is that you get some.

One Simple Thing You Can Do Every Day

When I'm feeling tense or stressed, I try to bring my anxiety levels down by focusing on my breathing. It takes only a few minutes and can be intensely calming. All you have to do is close your mouth (you want to breathe through your nose) and inhale deeply, filling up your diaphragm to its capacity. Hold it for a few seconds, and then slowly exhale. Repeat. I do this all the time—when I'm in traffic and running late, when I'm hanging out at home, when I'm mid-flight. It's very effective—and nobody will know what you're up to.

BEAUTY-REST TIPS

When it's time to settle down for the night, a racing brain is the hardest thing to control. If I'm feeling anxious, stressed out, or like there are a million things I should be doing instead of sleeping, it can take me the better part of an hour to fall asleep. To that end, I've developed a few handy tricks to ensure that when it's bedtime, it's truly time to go to sleep.

- I've banished the TV from my bedroom. It's just too tempting to turn it on, particularly when my mind doesn't feel ready to shut down for the night.

- I installed blackout shades to block out any light that might shine through my windows in the morning. A roll of kraft paper and some tape can easily create the same vibe.

- Count your blessings. Similar to the age-old method of counting sheep, some nights before drifting off I like to think of all the things I am thankful for.

- My mother always told me to keep a boring book by my bed. Think of falling asleep into your chemistry textbook the night before a test. Same concept.

- If all else fails, I will take a melatonin supplement. Melatonin is a hormone that our bodies produce to help us sleep. The supplements are natural and safe, but always talk to your doctor first to make sure it's something you should be taking, especially if you're younger than sixteen.

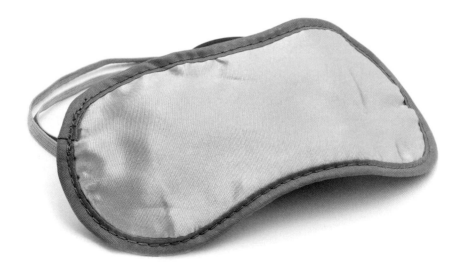

ME TIME AND DE-STRESSING

As the years have gone by, I've become increasingly comfortable with the concept of "me" time and that I need a fair amount of it. In fact, for the first time in my life, I'm living alone, and I kind of love it. I've always had roommates—which did have its pleasures—but now that it's just me and my dog, Chloe, I'm experiencing some of the upsides to living alone. It's healthy to be quiet and learn how to keep yourself company—and feel like you have the space to be contemplative. (Also, you are free to walk around in your underwear.) Plus it forces me to make actual plans to see my friends, and the time we spend together feels more concentrated and quality. (It's funny how you can live with people and still not really "see" them.)

If you share a house with your family, or live in a dorm with hundreds of others, it can feel impossible to find an inch of space that isn't otherwise occupied—whether it's by the physical presence, noises, or smells of strangers. And if you live in a city, it's not like you can escape the company of others by taking to the sidewalks! To that end, I've developed a handful of survival strategies for carving out the room to be by myself and de-stress, even when I spend a majority of my days surrounded by others.

- I keep headphones in my purse. If I'm at a photo shoot all day long, sometimes I need to find a corner, turn on some music, close my eyes, and pretend, for ten minutes, that I'm sitting on a beach somewhere. It's a little funny to think about now, but when I lived in San Francisco I used to just put on my headphones (sometimes without music) when I was walking down the street or the hallways between classes. This brief vacation is usually all I need to feel recharged—and if I'm clear that I just need a brief time-out, nobody finds it offensive or strange.

- I like taking Chloe for walks. We're not rushing to get somewhere specific; we're just strolling along. If time allows, I load her in the car and head out for a longer hike. Nature really is the best remedy.

- I schedule downtime. Silly, maybe, but if you specifically allot time for being lazy, you're less likely to feel guilty about it. And let's be honest: Every once in a while everyone needs a day, or at least an afternoon, when they don't have to do anything.

- Adopting a solo hobby is great. I love drawing, writing, and photography. There is something so nice about burying yourself in a project without a deadline.

Lesson Learned

When you're stressed, sometimes the best thing is to get a little perspective. It took me a long time to learn how to take a step back and look at the big picture, but when I did, it began to change the way I looked at things. In the past few years I've had the opportunity to travel all over the world, which has been totally eye-opening. Not being able to afford that new pair of Miu Miu platforms seems a lot less important when you are reminded that some go without shoes. Your boss giving you a hard time at work isn't as upsetting when you remember that there are those who can't find work at all. Perspective really is everything.

Instead of focusing on the problems that plague your life, try focusing on all the good. When I have had a tough day or week or even month, the thing that has always made me feel better is counting my blessings. Think of the people you love and the things in your life that make you happy. And if you are able to, try giving back. It doesn't have to be anything major. Not everyone can write a big check to a favorite charity, but most of us can volunteer an afternoon at a soup kitchen or donate some underused clothing to a local shelter.

- When I am traveling for work or book tours I make a date with myself. I used to attempt to burn the candle at both ends and would always end up so worn-out. For example, I travel to NYC for about four days every other month to work with my Kohl's design team. I used to schedule dinner and drinks every night I was there, because I have friends who I love to see when I'm in town. Combine late nights out with friends and ten-hour workdays in the Kohl's offices, and I would be exhausted halfway into my trip. I was unable to focus during meetings, and I was useless when it came to catching up with friends. Now I will make plans two of the evenings, and the other two nights I spend with room service and an overpriced hotel movie. I had to learn my happy medium between my work and my personal life or else both would suffer.

- Go for a thirty-minute run or bike ride. If I'm ever aggravated, frustrated, or just in a bad mood, this is the quickest way to turn my day around.

- Laughter—like laugh-so-hard-you-cry laughter—makes me happy, instantly. So I like to watch something funny. *Chelsea Lately* always makes me laugh or I'll look up funny videos on YouTube.

- That downtime I mentioned earlier? I'll usually whip up some sort of relaxing, hydrating mask and apply it (the best ones are tingly) before I pop in some DVDs of *Sex and the City*.

- Book a massage. You can find great deals at massage-therapy schools: Students need their practice and will happily practice on you for a super-low fee. These spots lack the frills of a spa (there's no lavender aromatherapy), but sometimes a fuss-free approach is the best anyway.

- Do my nails. I love nail art (wait until you get to chapter 11) and find painting my nails to be the best counterpart to TV-watching. It feels productive! I give myself a manicure about every other day.

CHAPTER FIVE
Fitness & Food

*I*n the past five years my weight hasn't changed drastically, but my attitude toward my body has. I used to think that if I looked thin that was all that mattered. I didn't think about how what I put into my body and what I put my body through was affecting me overall. But now I know that fitness and food aren't just about losing weight—they're part of a strong foundation for overall beauty. If you're good to your body, there's a better chance it will reward you with healthy skin and hair, higher energy, and a more positive attitude (which looks great on everyone).

My weight fluctuates from day to day, but I've pretty much been able to maintain a healthy goal weight without ever going to extremes. This isn't without some effort though: A few years ago my metabolism caught up with me, and I had to rethink what I should be eating every day and what qualifies as "exercise." In my early twenties I assumed that if I went for a fifteen-minute walk, I could absolutely justify a few slices of pizza. In my mid-twenties I had to come to terms with the basic math of matching calories consumed with calories burned. I have a handle on it now, which I can chalk up to three things:

1. I understand what I should be eating and what I should be eating only occasionally.

2. I've figured out a way to incorporate exercise into my everyday life.

3. I've learned that when I embrace moderation, my body is at its healthiest.

As you probably know from reading practically any article about dieting, extreme dieting can mess with your metabolism. So, while I might cut back on carbohydrates and schedule a few extra workouts before a cover shoot, I never starve myself.

This is not to say that it's easy to keep your head about your body shape, but just as you can't will yourself to grow three inches, you can't will yourself to have a slimmer waist or curvier hips. I'd be lying if I didn't say that there are things that bug me about my body, even though I can acknowledge that my concerns can be a bit delusional and body-dysmorphic. But that's how it goes in Hollywood, where there is constant pressure to be thin. I try to be extra-conscious of this and keep my eye on what is realistic, healthy, and unchangeable about the build of my body. I'm never going to have the thinnest thighs. I've accepted this. And I've learned that it's essential to respect my body and what it needs. It needs to eat clean, healthy food; it needs water; and it needs to move. Once I instituted good habits, my body came to expect and even enjoy them. I still indulge though—I eat things that aren't great for me (but taste so good!), and I skip workouts to hang out with friends or get an extra hour of sleep. Nobody's perfect, and you shouldn't feel like you have to be. The best life is a balanced life. So enjoy the good-for-you and the bad-for-you, all in moderation.

FITNESS

Growing up, I was always very active and involved in sports. I played soccer from kindergarten until I graduated from high school. I've also played tennis since I was young, and I still manage to get out on the court when I can find the time (although my forehand isn't what it used to be). It's funny now to look back at soccer practice, when I used to glare angrily at my coach for adding extra sprints to the end of our scrimmages. These days I'm lined up outside a Barry's Bootcamp class thirty minutes early, fighting for a treadmill and an overly vocal trainer to do the exact same thing . . . and now I'm *paying* for it (and scrambling for ways to fit it into my schedule). Sometimes it's hard to find that hour in a day you can devote to exercise. We are all guilty of letting our jobs, homework, relationships, and other responsibilities come before our physical health, but staying fit is an important responsibility to yourself. Your health affects everything, from your energy to your brain function to your mood to your skin. Incorporating exercise into your regular routine will ultimately pay off—try to do at least thirty minutes of exercise four days a week. Schedule the time, like you would with any other activity in your life. It's not just your body that responds positively to moderate exercise; your mind will benefit too. Try a kickboxing class at the end of a long, hard day and tell me that you don't feel infinitely better.

Finding an exercise plan that works with your schedule—and sticking to it—can be challenging. Here are some tips that get me out the door—or at least moving.

- If you're not a fan of intense exercise (e.g., running or spinning), consider investing in a pedometer in order to track your steps every day. Set a reasonable goal and then make yourself walk until you meet it.

- I'm a big fan of group exercise. I always have my best success sticking to an exercise plan when I'm either meeting a friend at the gym or going to a class

One Simple Thing You Can Do Every Day

You don't have to run ten miles and exist entirely on beauty power foods to feel like you've done something good to take care of yourself. Find the balance: Try to either eat reasonably well all day or get some real exercise. And remember: It's never too late to turn the page on what might be a morning full of theoretical diet disasters. (We all have those run-ins with Dunkin' Donuts.) Go for a brisk walk before bed and you can go to sleep resting easy.

Also be sure to drink enough water. The jury will always be out on whether eight glasses per day is just right, too little, or too much, but give your digestive system a hand by taking in enough fluids. It's usually the function that suffers when you're a bit dehydrated.

that's scheduled in my calendar. (If you're really flaky about working out, book a class with strict cancellation policies.)

- Music can be a huge motivator, particularly if you're struggling through a long run. If I'm excited to hear a complete playlist, it can be everything in getting me through to the end. Sometimes, if I feel like quitting or slowing down, I'll make myself run until the end of a song (and then the end of the next one . . .). Music with a strong, steady beat will help keep you moving.

- Get outside. A three-hour hike with a good friend is a great way to catch up—and break a sweat. Same with a day at the slopes or a bike ride along the beach. These sorts of activities are generally so enjoyable that you'll barely notice how hard you're working. The other great upside of exercising outside is that you're challenging your body to react to the obstacles in its path, which can be more effective than running on the treadmill day after day.

- Build up an exercise-DVD library. As funny as it might feel to work out in your living room, I love an old-school workout video for those days when I'm just not motivated to make it to the gym. I generally look for videos that focus more on stretching and toning rather than jumping around. (I am sure my downstairs neighbor appreciates this.) Some of my favorite series include the Tracy Anderson Method and Barry's Bootcamp.

- Take the stairs. My mother always used to do this, and I thought it was so funny, but it works. Look for any other reasonable opportunity to move just a little bit, even if it's only taking the long way to the bathroom or parking at the far end of the lot. All those little walks add up. If you live within a couple miles of your school or work, leave a little earlier and walk there instead of driving (good for you and good for the environment).

EATING RIGHT

I used to eat way too much. And I used to eat terrible things. I really didn't know enough about food, so I relied on things that were processed and often frozen (not that all frozen food is bad, but if you can primarily eat things that are fresh it's a good start). I never had any energy, I didn't feel good, and I didn't look that good either. So I started to read books about proper diet, learned more about nutrition, and asked pointed questions of my doctors, and eventually I got myself back on track. When we're young, we usually have the metabolism to support some pretty bad habits, but I've definitely noticed that as I age I need to pay closer attention to what I eat. Dessert every night? It just doesn't fly anymore.

Eating healthfully consistently takes preparation and forethought and can be really difficult, unless you live in the center of a farm-to-market, foodie town or happen to have an expansive vegetable garden in your backyard. As one of the few things in life that's within our control, deciding what to eat can quickly become an obsession, particularly once you begin to learn about what might be lurking in processed food. While I absolutely think that mindful consumption is the way to go, you're only setting yourself up for failure if you try to be completely healthy all the time. I aim for 75 percent super-healthy, 20 percent decent, and 5 percent decadent, and figure that those sorts of odds will still put me ahead.

I try to resist fad diets. I don't believe in them. If it's important, for health reasons, that you lose weight, choose an approach that's actually a lifestyle—one that feels fully and happily maintainable. You need to find the patience to slowly whittle your waistline down. Don't rush to shed the weight in record time, or you'll regain it just as quickly.

In the last few years I have really taken an interest in the types of foods I put into my body and the effect they have on me. Everyone seems to have an opinion on what foods are essential and whether things like gluten are going to kill you in your sleep—it's often so excessive that you can read an article or see a documentary and walk away wondering if *anything* is safe to eat. While I definitely focus on a narrower range of foods (I maintain a mostly pescatarian diet), I try not to drive myself insane with food paranoia.

There is no universally perfect diet—we all react to different foods in different ways, so the best way to find what works for you is to try new things. Try eating a salad with dinner more often or cut out processed sugar or simple carbohydrates for a few weeks. Make a conscious effort to choose water instead of soda (yes, even diet soda). Changes like these can have a big impact on your overall health. And now that I've trained my body to crave good foods, I don't want the bad things as much anymore. I legitimately crave vegetables. I don't drink my coffee with cream and sugar anymore. (I forced myself to acquire the taste for drinking it black, and now actually prefer it.)

BEAUTY POWER FOODS AND VITAMINS

Those rumors that B vitamins strengthen and lengthen your hair, that vitamin E improves the health of your nails, and that vitamin A makes skin look younger and dewier? In my experience, they are all true. There are a whole host of power foods that can provide all sorts of antiaging, skin-energizing results. These foods are the most expedient and natural way to introduce vitamins into your system—you can take supplements, but certain vitamins are toxic if you take too many, so it's best to let your body draw what it needs out of the foods you eat. Turn the page for a chart of vitamins and nutrients and what they're good for.

NUTRIENT	WHAT IT'S GOOD FOR	WHERE YOU CAN FIND IT
VITAMIN A	Gives you dewy, even-toned skin and a healthy scalp. It also helps maintain your eyesight.	Cantaloupe, grapefruit, apricots, carrots, broccoli, sweet potatoes, kale, spinach, pumpkin, eggs.
VITAMIN B	Prevents your skin from becoming too oily and decreases breakouts. B vitamins also boost your metabolism and can help improve the quality of hair, skin, and muscle tone.	Bananas, poultry, tuna, shellfish, avocados, beans, nuts, eggs, milk, whole grains.
VITAMIN C	Diminishes the appearance of scars, cuts, and bruises; boosts collagen production, which is good for your skin; and fuels your immune system.	Citrus fruits, berries, apples, melon, pineapples, tomatoes, spinach, cabbage, red and green peppers, broccoli, Brussels sprouts, cauliflower.
VITAMIN D	Helps combat dry skin and is important for the development of healthy teeth and bones.	You can get the "sunshine" vitamin by spending 10–15 minutes three times a week in the sunlight—without sunscreen on. It can also be found in fortified milk and other dairy products, tuna, and salmon.
VITAMIN E	Gives you healthy skin and minimizes scars, burns, inflammations, and irritations. Vitamin E is also an antioxidant, so it helps with dry, flaky skin and protects the skin from damage.	Fruit juices, spinach, asparagus, broccoli, nuts, nut oils.

NUTRIENT	WHAT IT'S GOOD FOR	WHERE YOU CAN FIND IT
VITAMIN K	Helps combat dark under-eye circles.	Kale, spinach, turnip greens, collard greens, Swiss chard, mustard greens, parsley, romaine, green leaf lettuce, Brussels sprouts, broccoli, cauliflower, cabbage.
ANTIOXIDANTS	Repairs or prevents skin damage.	All foods containing vitamins A, C, E.
FLAVONOIDS	Improve the quality of your skin and give it a glowing appearance. These are antioxidants.	Apples, all citrus fruits, berries, tea (white and green), dark chocolate, celery, onions, kale, parsley, soybeans, tomatoes, eggplant.
OMEGA-3 FATTY ACIDS	Contributes to shiny, conditioned hair.	Soybeans, flaxseeds, walnuts, Brussels sprouts, kale, spinach, salad greens, salmon, tuna.

Detoxing and Cleansing

Occasionally I like to do a low-key detox (especially after the holidays). Sometimes I'll just cut out processed sugar, simple carbs, caffeine, and alcohol for a couple weeks, and other times I'll do a three- or five-day cleanse, consuming only juices and vegan, raw food. Doing a cleanse is a great way to give your digestive system a break and recharge your mind. But if you're going to detox, be responsible about it and make sure you get the calories and nutrients you need. (You might want to do a cleanse through a company that provides all the juices—if so, be sure it's a reputable company.) And make sure you're prepared. It's important to eat healthfully before beginning a cleanse, and the same rule applies to completing one. (See the Lesson Learned on page 73 for why.)

BEAUTY
ON THE ROAD

When I'm traveling—which happens with a fair amount of frequency—it can be nearly impossible to maintain my routine. No surprise there: Travel is stressful, from the anxiety of the trip itself (airports, security lines, long delays), to the change in time zone, to the fact that you're apart from your loved ones and the things that bring you comfort throughout the day—from the kinds of food you normally eat, to your beauty and fitness rituals. (Don't get me wrong: When I'm going to a warm, tropical destination for vacation, I don't find it stressful at all.)

For skin, what proves most disruptive is not the dry airplane air (though it is dehydrating) but the shift in products. For example, you might not pack your normal shampoo and instead use whatever the hotel provides; that shampoo comes in direct contact with your face. I always used to forget my cleanser and would use bar soap instead. Not so great for your skin. These days I travel so often that I keep a bag of permanently packed toiletries in my suitcase with travel-size versions of everything, from my favorite exfoliator to my moisturizer and conditioner. If you can't find travel sizes of your products (sites like minimus.biz specialize in this), stock up on the convenient mini bottles from the Container Store. A little extra effort can really benefit your skin, especially if you fly often. Meanwhile, when it comes to cosmetics, make sure that when you're buying your products at the makeup counter, you ask for samples of all of your purchases. It's so much better than running around trying to find your product (or having to test something new while you're far away from home)!

When it comes to keeping my diet and fitness routines on track, I try not to be too militant about it. I know that life is about moderation and that a few days off from my normal exercise and diet routines isn't going to send me up a dress size. If I'm going to be on the road for more than a few days, and won't have access to a gym, I have a simple exercise routine that my trainer Jarett Del Bene helped me develop. It can be done using just what's in your hotel room. I usually do three to five sets of the following circuit:

- 50 jumping jacks

- 20 squat jumps

- 20 push-ups

- 30 lunges (alternating legs and being careful to not overextend your knee)

- 25 curls using water bottles as weights

- 25 squats while holding a water bottle in each hand

- 25 dips (using a chair to support yourself)

Or, if the weather permits, I'll find thirty minutes to an hour to go for a brisk walk, which is one of the best ways to get to know a city. When it comes to food, I try to seek out the healthiest options (this can be hard, particularly in airports), but I don't beat myself up if nothing is available. (Yes, I've been known to indulge in the occasional salted pretzel.) I usually tote around some Luna, KIND, or Kashi snack bars in my purse, so I'm not stuck in front of a vending machine weighing my only options. And while it isn't the most exciting option, most coffee shops will usually have apples or bananas.

CHAPTER SIX
Makeup Tips, Tricks, and Techniques

alking into the beauty department of any store can be overwhelming. With makeup palettes that span the entire rainbow, countless brushes offered in every shape and size, and a sea of cosmetics and scents, it can leave a girl wondering where to even begin. Which products do you actually need and which will you be persuaded to buy only to then gather dust at the bottom of your makeup drawer? (Teal mascara? What was I thinking?) The whole experience can be a little much, unless you go in there armed with some beauty know-how and information about the essential products and tools.

That's why this chapter is all about the basics—the useful tips and the necessary tools that will prepare you to be a makeup pro. The pages that follow pretty much sum up everything I've learned about makeup over the years (most of it thanks to my talented makeup artist and dear friend, Amy Nadine Rosenberg). Once you've got the basics down, you'll be ready to have more fun with everyday looks and makeup for parties and events.

ABOUT FACE

Get to know the features on your face and the terms used in this guide by referring to this annotated picture.

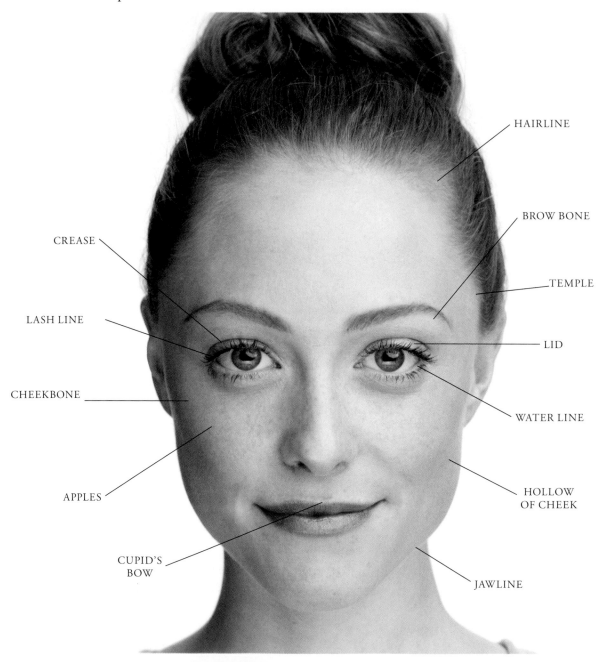

HAIRLINE

BROW BONE

TEMPLE

CREASE

LASH LINE

LID

CHEEKBONE

WATER LINE

APPLES

HOLLOW OF CHEEK

CUPID'S BOW

JAWLINE

PRODUCTS

Before you can learn how best to apply makeup, you have to make sure you have the right materials for the job. Everyone's key products will be different, so experimenting with a variety of options will help you build a collection that properly suits your needs. Things like your skin type and complexion will be the deciding factor for some choices, but your personal preference will figure in, too. For example, not everyone likes the way they look with blush or bronzer on . . . and that's okay. Your perfect products should reflect both what works best *on* you and *for* you. But just as important as finding those products is knowing how to use them. After all, the greatest beauty products in the world won't do you much good if you don't know how to apply them.

What Makeup Can Do for You

Through years of trial and error (and, of course, with help from Amy Nadine), I have learned exactly what makeup can do for my face and which products work best for me. But I want you to see for yourself the subtle—but often powerful—effect makeup can have, so the following pages are filled with images that demonstrate this. It may seem obvious, but the impact of a simple before-and-after cannot be underestimated. You might see something in here you'd previously written off—and it could change your whole look. Plus I've included information about each product to help you start compiling a list of your everyday makeup essentials (for mine, see page 118).

FOUNDATION

BEFORE

AFTER

If the word "foundation" makes you think of caked-on makeup, try a few different kinds before you rule it out—formulas today tend to be lightweight while still delivering the illusion of flawless skin. And that's really the point of foundation—not to look like you have layers of makeup on but to help your skin look its best. There are three basic types to choose from: powder, liquid, and cream. Powder is good if your skin tends to be oily, and cream works best on skin that is on the drier side. All skin types can benefit from liquid foundation. If you still think foundation is not for you, you can substitute it with a tinted moisturizer—it won't offer as much coverage, but it will provide a nice base—or a lightweight foundation. Only go for a heavier foundation if your skin truly warrants it.

Application Tips:
- If your skin is dry and flake-prone, exfoliate in the morning, not only so that your moisturizer can get in but also so that your foundation doesn't accentuate the flakes on your face.
- Never apply foundation to unmoisturized skin. The jury is still out on whether primer is truly necessary (save money and skip it), but the skin should be prepped in some way—Amy Nadine does this with moisturizing serum.
- If your skin is oily, choose an oil-free foundation (same goes for if you're going to be somewhere hot and humid).
- Be sure to warm foundation in the palm of your hand (a small amount, maybe the size of a quarter) before you sweep it across your face and neck. You can use a foundation brush, but as long as your hands are clean, they're the best at getting at hard-to-reach places.
- A trick for finding the right shade of foundation is to match it to your chest, particularly if you're good at protecting your face and neck with sunscreen. You don't want your face to look pale compared to your body. And don't rely on store lighting—check out the color in daylight before you decide if it's a match.
- Don't forget about where your jawline meets your neck! Make sure that your face and neck match by blending the foundation into the top of your neck as well.
- Dust powder across your forehead, nose, and chin to set the foundation.

CONCEALER

BEFORE

AFTER

This offers a big assist to your foundation in completely evening out your skin tone and addressing problem areas. It comes in various forms—pencils, creams, sticks—and you'll want to do some experimenting to see which you prefer. Amy Nadine suggests a stick or a cream for blemishes. You should choose a color that matches your skin (versus under-eye concealer, which should be slightly lighter).

Application Tips:
- Dab on concealer with either your fingertip or a small, firm brush (don't rub), and use as little as possible so that it doesn't get cakey.
- Follow it with an extra dusting of powder to make sure it stays put.
- If you're covering up a whitehead, see page 144.

READER Q: HOW DO I STOP FLAKY SKIN FROM SHOWING THROUGH?

Not only does dry skin tend to show through foundation, it makes it difficult to get foundation to adhere properly. When I'm battling flakes before an event or photo shoot, and exfoliating with a gentle scrub or brush isn't enough, Amy Nadine will dab a small amount of petroleum-based ointment onto the problem area and then apply the foundation. Save it for emergencies because it can cause breakouts, but it totally works in a sticky situation!

UNDER-EYE CONCEALER

BEFORE

AFTER

Some people find that they just can't avoid dark under-eye circles even when they're managing nine hours of sleep a night. Sometimes it simply comes down to genetics. For under-eye concealer, you'll need something creamy, since the area around your eye doesn't produce oil (don't use under-eye concealer on your face, and vice versa), and you'll want a shade slightly lighter than your skin (but not too light!). I used to only use under-eye concealer until Amy Nadine taught me that sometimes highlighting powder can provide the same effect.

Application Tips:

- Apply your under-eye concealer after you have completed your eyes, since it will pick up any fallen makeup.
- Using your fingertip, a sponge, or a flat synthetic-bristled concealer brush, warm up the product on the back of your hand before you place it in the center of your under-eye area.
- Amy Nadine's method is to start from the center to ensure complete coverage, so using small strokes in a stippling motion, move from the center toward the inner corner of the eye; then head back to the center and to the outer corner.
- Immediately after applying, brush loose or pressed powder to "set" the concealer in place, then use a sponge to sweep extra powder away.

BRONZER

BEFORE   AFTER

Instead of relying on the sun for that summertime glow try looking to bronzer—it can deliver the same effect, and what's even better is that you have much more control over the result. Avoid anything orange and go for something that looks light brown or taupe. You might require two shades—one for winter and one for summer, when your skin tends to naturally get darker. Use a big, soft Kabuki-style brush when applying.

Application Tips:

- Suck in your cheeks to find exactly where your cheekbones are located. You want to sweep the bronzer across the hollows of your cheeks and along your cheekbones, starting on the outside of your apples and following the bone all the way to your ears.

- You can also apply bronzer on your temples, hairline, along the sides of your nose, and under your jawline in light, circular motions. If you do, make sure to brush your neck with bronzer too. (You don't want a line there.)

- To make it look natural, Amy Nadine taught me to go back over the bronzed areas with the same brush, though this time with some translucent powder. Swirl the brush around until there are no lines between the bronzed and unbronzed skin.

BLUSH

BEFORE   AFTER

This is the quickest way to looking flushed and healthy—it truly warms up your entire face. Even though the mention of blush probably makes you think of powder and a brush, blush also comes in a cream. Both forms are great choices. Powder is best for beginners and lasts longer, while cream blush is a good choice for drier skin.

Application Tips:

- Smile in the mirror to find the apples of your cheeks—they're the high, round parts that appear more prominently when you smile—and focus your efforts there.
- If you're new to blush, start with an apricot or peachy shade (always go slightly more orange than you think, since it translates as pink on the cheek).
- In general, you're looking for a color that looks natural on you, like a healthy flush.
- If you have dark skin, choose a brighter color, because lighter colors won't show up as well.
- Make sure your blush and lip color don't clash. Try selecting both from the same color family.

EYELINER

BEFORE

AFTER

This accentuates the natural shape of the eye and can add instant definition and drama. If you're feeling tired, sometimes a little eyeliner is all it takes to make your eyes appear more awake. The variety of ways to line your eyes is sort of endless—you can use pencils (kohl or kajal), liquid, eye shadow and a wet brush, gel and a brush . . . You can line above your lash line or inside the rim; you can apply a thin line or a thick line . . . and so on. Experiment to see what works best for you and is within your skill level.

Application Tips:

- Don't go straight at your eye with the pencil or wand—hold it at an angle and drag it across the lid to create the smoothest line possible.
- Keep your liner right up against your lashes, just at the lash line.
- If you apply black eyeliner pencil to the inner rim of your eye, it can make your eye color look more piercing. But don't do this if you're worried about making your eyes appear smaller, since this can close up the eye. Lining your inner rim in white or a nude tone will make the eye appear more open.
- If your eyeliner tends to smudge easily, it could be because your lids are oily (which means that while you might have a hard time keeping your eyeliner on, your eyes will stay young-looking longer!). Sweep some light-colored eye shadow or powder across your lids for a drier surface before you apply liner.

The Eyeliner Effect

The following images are all of my eye with different eyeliner in each shot. (The first image is no eyeliner.) Look at how different styles of eyeliner can change the shape of your eye.

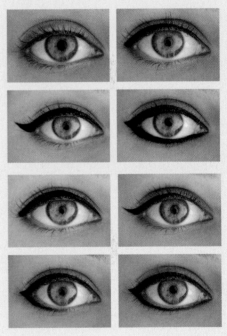

MASCARA

BEFORE

AFTER

There's no single product—besides, maybe, red lipstick—that delivers a bigger "looking finished" effect. You generally have to choose between regular and waterproof mascara, but you should only use waterproof mascara (and liner) on special occasions, because they tend to dry out the skin around your eyes, speeding up the aging process. Different formulas provide different effects—some will give your lashes a more defined look while others leave your lashes looking softer.

Application Tips:
- Choose a formula that's nonclumping and natural-looking and then use the wand in both combing and wiggling motions, horizontally and vertically.
- Don't pump the wand in an attempt to get more mascara on the brush. This pushes air into the tube, which will dry out your mascara faster.
- When Amy Nadine does my makeup she spends about thirty seconds brushing my lashes from every angle: It's the best way for reaching and defining each and every lash.
- If you have very light lashes, mascara should definitely be one of your everyday essentials. If black feels too dramatic for you try a dark brown instead.

EYE SHADOW

BEFORE

AFTER

I don't wear a lot of eye shadow (if I do it's usually a neutral color, sometimes with a bit of shimmer), but it looks great on a lot of women and can add complexity and depth to the eye. It's also a nice way to add a pop of color to your face. It comes in both powder and cream forms. I prefer a powder over a cream because cream shadows tend to crease with time. For day choose a matte shade; for night have fun and try a metallic or shimmery shade.

Application Tips:

- Use an eye-shadow brush to apply an even layer across the lid.
- For extra drama go one shade darker in the crease, making sure to blend it well. When you use more than one color you never want to see a distinct line.

READER Q: HOW OFTEN SHOULD I REPLACE MY MAKEUP?

I replace my mascara and liner every three months (they're particularly susceptible to bacteria) and anything else that's liquid (foundation, etc.) every six months. For things that are powdery, I usually go through them before they need to be tossed, although if I use them infrequently I get rid of them after they've hung around for two years. Ultimately use common sense: If something smells or looks strange, or has completely changed color, don't put it on your face!

EYEBROW POWDER/PENCIL

BEFORE

AFTER

This adds instant polish, fills in any spare patches, and only takes a few seconds to do. There are special "brow powders" out there, but really they're just eye shadow marketed as brow powder. For a softer look use a powder. For a more defined look try an eyebrow pencil.

Application Tips:

- Unless you are going for a dramatic effect, don't go any darker than your own brow color, since the goal here is not to change the shade but simply to correct any imperfections.
- Use an eyebrow-specific brush (which has short, stiff, angled bristles) or a pencil and work out to the tip with small strokes. Always follow the direction of hair growth. Stand about a foot away from the mirror so you can get some perspective on the whole operation.

LIPSTICK/LIP GLOSS

BEFORE

AFTER

It's no secret what a bold-colored lipstick can do for you, but it doesn't come without a price. A dramatic lip color is arguably the most high-maintenance look a girl can wear on her face, which means it should be reserved for special occasions. Fortunately even just a subtle pop of color can elevate your look. When you're picking out a lipstick, you can choose between matte or satin, and each gives a different effect. Same goes for lip gloss—you can pick one in a bold color or something more sheer. And don't feel like you need to spend a fortune on just one—drugstore lipsticks and glosses are as good as the pricey ones and come in so many colors and finishes. Buy a bunch so you have a variety to choose from.

Application Tips:

- Make sure your lips are moisturized. Chapped lips are not the place for lipstick. If your lips are too dry, you're better off with tinted lip balm or lip gloss.
- If you want to use liner to define the shape of your lips, pick a color that either matches your lips or if you're using lipstick then the shade you've chosen.
- Although I'm a fan of metaphorically coloring outside the lines, this is definitely not the place for it. Follow the natural shape of your mouth or else you'll risk looking like you've escaped from the circus. (If you have thin lips, turn to page 144 for tips on how to make them look fuller.)
- After you've applied your lipstick, blot with a tissue to even out the color.
- If you need your lipstick to last, apply one coat, follow that with a dusting of translucent powder, then apply another coat of color.

TOOLS

Having the right makeup won't get you anywhere if you don't have the tools to apply it. So make sure you've got what you need.

THE TOOLS I TURN TO EVERY DAY

I do a lot of test-driving, but unlike with makeup, where new products are constantly replacing old favorites, my collection of tools remains pretty much the same.

SPONGES

I usually apply my foundation with my fingertips or a brush, but I do love Amy Nadine's trusted egg-shaped blender sponge. It's particularly handy for blending foundation around the inner eyes and around the nose, plus if you wet the sponge first, the foundation will go on more sheerly.

TWEEZERS

Make sure you have high-quality tweezers. Cheap tweezers will only lead to frustration. You'll need a pair with a flat, angled edge for minor brow touch-ups. For more on brow shaping, see page 108.

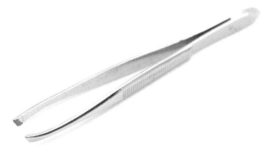

COTTON SWABS

Using a cotton swab is the quickest way to perfect eyeliner or clean up any eye makeup that has gravitated to your cheeks (which, by the way, is one of the reasons that, if eye shadow is involved, it makes sense to complete your eyes before moving on to the rest of your face).

EYELASH CURLER

Curling your lashes opens up your eye, and it's a subtle, pretty effect to have your lashes flare out from your lids. If you wear glasses and have straight lashes, you should definitely learn how to use a curler to avoid that annoying feeling of something touching the edges of your lashes all day. (Turn to page 127 for help with a curler.)

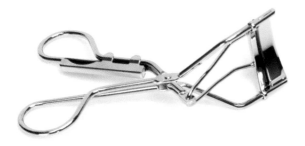

BRUSHES

Good brushes—i.e., brushes that you can keep forever if you take good care of them—can be expensive, so I recommend building your collection little by little until you have everything you need. These brushes are going to be used directly on your skin, so make sure that they feel soft rather than scratchy (although some brushes should be firm, depending on their use). You don't need to buy the most expensive brushes out there to achieve the desired effect. For some, yes, it's worth spending a little extra—if you're going to splurge, do it on a soft powder brush. But honestly, all price ranges offer brushes to get the job done. The more expensive ones just feel

Keeping Your Tools Clean

Be sure to wash your brushes (and sponges) gently with mild soap and warm water every week (or after every use if you have acne-prone skin). There are specific brush cleansers out on the market, but they're really not necessary. Mild soap and water will do just fine. Lay your brushes flat to dry on your counter. For natural-fiber brushes, try to keep the washing action close to the tip, since water at the base can loosen the hairs and make them fall out.

better and will last longer. Brushes are often identified as "synthetic" or "natural," and you'll want a combination of the two in your collection. Synthetic brushes are said to be best for cream blushes and shadows while natural brushes are best for powders. But professionals break those rules all the time, so you can too.

There are over thirty different makeup-brush shapes out on the market (and then variations within that, depending on the brand), but you don't even need to know about all of them unless you're considering a profession in makeup. You can get by with owning only a handful. Here are the basics:

FOUNDATION: A synthetic brush. Can also be used for applying cream blush.

CONCEALER: A narrow, synthetic brush with a slightly tapered edge.

POWDER: A big, soft natural-fiber brush.

CONTOURING: A soft brush with a flat, angled edge. Also used for bronzing.

BLUSH: A soft medium-full round brush. Natural-fiber is best.

EYE SHADOW: A tapered flat brush that is good for blending.

FAN BRUSH: A light brush that's great for highlighter. (It's also good for brushing away loose eye shadow.)

EYELINER: A narrow, angled brush for applying a gel liner or shadow as liner.

EYELASH AND BROW COMB: The side with a small, plastic comb is used for removing mascara clumps from lashes. The bristled side is for grooming eyebrows. (You can also use a spoolie brush.)

EYEBROW: A firm, angled brush used for filling in with brow powder. Go for something with coarser bristles.

FACE PREP:
HOW TO SHAPE YOUR BROWS

You know those people who don't pay much attention to their eyeglasses and are always a little surprised when you remind them that they're the first thing others see? The same can be said of eyebrows. They seem like background and are often overlooked, but they're a critical feature: They provide much of the essential architecture of your face and should be strong, defined, and clean. But natural! You never want to turn your brows into something they're not; your best look will probably mean working with the brow shape you were born with. Sometimes subtle tweaks like simply cleaning up below the brow can make a big difference; other times you might need to opt for some more serious pruning. (*Nobody* looks cute with a unibrow.)

Finding your arch can be difficult. I strongly recommend booking an appointment with a trusted eyebrow guru (ask your friends for a recommendation) and then being diligent about maintaining the lines the specialist sets. This is much less risky than doing your own shaping from the beginning. I tend to have a strong reaction to wax, so I go to someone who only uses tweezers. This takes longer and is more painful, but it's worth it to me.

If you are going to take on this task yourself, follow these steps for narrowing in on your arches. You can also invest in a brow kit that provides stencils (but I would still run through these steps to match it up).

1. Take a pencil and hold it vertically against your nose. Where it hits your eyebrow is where the brow should begin (anything leftover in the middle is your unibrow and is fair game for plucking). Mark the end of your brow with your eyebrow pencil or eyeliner as a line that's not to be crossed.

2. Starting from the same position as in step one, tilt the pencil directly across the center of your eye on the diagonal. The spot where it hits your brow is your arch. Mark it with the brow pencil or eyeliner.

3. Now tilt the pencil so the tip aligns with the outer edge of your eye. Where it hits is the end of your brow. Mark it with a pencil.

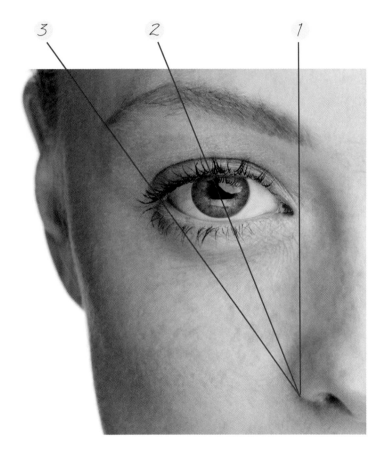

NOW IT'S TIME TO GET PLUCKING:

1. Using your tweezers, pluck any hairs that are clearly well outside of the confines of your brow. Remember to keep a light hand: You want those

Lesson Learned

When I was in high school I sat behind a girl who always came to class late and frantic to finish her makeup each day. Seriously this girl always had about half of her face incomplete, and that included her eyebrows . . . because she had yet to draw them on. If you're too young to recall this time (or have mentally blocked it out), there was a trend to either wax or shave off your eyebrows and then draw them back on. Scary, but true! Anyway, I would watch, completely entertained, as she quickly drew them on every day before the teacher began class. The funny thing was that their shape and size varied day to day. And depending on their angle, she appeared to have a different expression each morning. Think of how a cartoon character is drawn. Eyebrows slanted down and in makes an angry face. Eyebrows arched and drawn slightly higher implies surprise. And so on. In case the moral of this story isn't clear: Eyebrow shape is pretty key to your appearance. (Second moral: Don't shave off your eyebrows!)

guys to look full and natural. And pluck from underneath the hair and in the direction it grows.

2. If your eyebrow hairs are long, you can take a brow brush and comb them straight up. Trim the bits that go beyond the brow line with cuticle scissors or embroidery scissors. Be careful not to cut too much!

Make no mistake: Eyebrow upkeep can be tricky. It's easy to lose perspective when those tweezers are in your hand and your face is pressed up against the mirror. You can go way too far in just a few seconds. The same can also happen when you're trying to "even out" your work. Overplucking can lead to permanent damage. (Sometimes eyebrow hairs don't grow back at all.) Before you get pluck happy, pledge to only tug out one hair at a time—and to constantly take two steps back from the mirror to assess your progress.

If you color your hair regularly, you can ask your colorist to match your brow color with your base color.

BEAUTY CRIMES

Don't get caught in the act of a crime against beauty! We did some time for it so you won't have to. . . .

RACCOON EYES

Unless you want to look like you slept in your makeup (all week), please don't do this.

MESSY LIPSTICK

That shade looks great on your lips . . . not your teeth.

WRONG SHADE OF FOUNDATION

Using foundation on your face that doesn't match the rest of your body is a rookie mistake. If you are going to take the time to apply it, make sure it matches and is properly blended.

TOO-DARK LIP LINER

Wearing a lip liner that is much darker than your lip color is never a good look. If you aren't going to match your liner, skip it altogether.

OVER-BRONZING

Too much bronzer can take you from looking sun-kissed to looking sun-damaged.

OUT-OF-CONTROL BANGS

Bangs aren't for everyone. If you have a great head of curls, why mess with nature? If you must have them then make sure you're ready to commit to daily styling.

WEARING TOO MUCH MAKEUP

Remember that when it comes to beauty, less is more, and more is . . . tacky.

VISIBLE DRY SHAMPOO

This is far worse than dirty hair. Always be sure to blend.

OVER-ACCESSORIZING

Adding a little something extra to your hair can be cute, but don't go crazy. Wearing too many accessories can ruin a good hairstyle.

CHAPTER SEVEN

Everyday Makeup

I rarely leave home without at least a little makeup on. I just don't feel comfortable unless I have even the most minimal coverage on my face. (I do also run a greater-than-average risk of being photographed and having pictures of me show up online or in magazines.) Besides, the ritual of applying my makeup is like my ten minutes of quiet mental prep for the day ahead.

But as dependent as I may be on some lightweight foundation and mascara, I know my limits: Amy Nadine has ensured that I'm well-trained in keeping my makeup subtle during daylight hours. Let's put it this way: You would most definitely recognize me if you saw me first thing in the morning.

I guess that's really the thing: Everyday makeup should even out your skin tone, conceal any unsightlies, and subtly enhance your features. In other words, it should just make you look like a slightly more polished, more flawless version of yourself.

MY EVERYDAY MAKEUP ESSENTIALS

I like to try out as many new products as possible in the never-ending quest for finding the best beauty products out there, so I have what amounts to a library of makeup. But I've learned the hard way that I really need to edit down to the essentials to help get me out the door in a timely manner (or to lighten my luggage while traveling). Which means I always have the following items set aside on my vanity to achieve my everyday look. While they are in order of appearance, I'm not going to give you specific brands, because they are constantly changing. I'm always finding a new formula I prefer or a new all-natural product to try. The list of ingredients to avoid on page 24 will help guide you to the best products. (And I often list my favorite products of the moment on my website, www.laurenconrad.com.)

1. SPF AND MOISTURIZER: Before I apply my makeup, I clean, tone, and moisturize my face. And then I apply a healthy layer of SPF. My moisturizer doesn't have SPF, so I apply them separately, but there are a lot of great moisturizers that do also have SPF.

2. LIGHTWEIGHT FOUNDATION: Since I try to go as bare as possible during the day so that my makeup isn't visible, I use a lightweight liquid foundation. (Some of these come with SPF too.) If my skin is particularly clear, I'll cut my foundation with a little moisturizer for coverage that's a bit more sheer.

3. CONCEALER: Once my foundation is on, I go back in with concealer and a brush to dab out any redness (dot, don't rub). Don't try to cover your blemishes with foundation; it will be much too thick.

4. UNDER-EYE CONCEALER: I also keep a stick or pot of under-eye concealer on hand in case I'm dealing with some dark circles. I use different

kinds, depending on the day. One day I might opt for the stick for heavier coverage, and the next a liquid tube is enough. Face concealer and under-eye concealer are very different: The skin around your eyes doesn't produce oil, so concealer for it is much silkier.

5. HIGHLIGHTER: I brighten the area right under my eyes (above the cheek-bone, but more on that on page 142), which automatically makes me look like I got three extra hours of sleep. Brilliant.

6. BRONZER: I use this to add a sun-kissed touch and for subtle contouring (more on this too on page 142).

7. BLUSH: I use a powder blush, and it goes right on the apples of my cheeks for a natural flush of color.

8. LIQUID EYELINER: It's a favorite and always will be. I never feel like myself without a swipe of liquid eyeliner winged out and up on my lid. I apply a thinner line during the day and a thicker, more dramatic one for the night.

9. SKIN-TONE EYE SHADOW: I don't wear colored eye shadow as a general rule because it makes me feel too "done up," but I do apply either a powder that matches my skin tone or a neutral-colored shadow to my lid in order to ensure that my liner doesn't travel.

10. TRANSLUCENT POWDER: A light dusting locks in my foundation so that it lasts hours longer and keeps my T-zone from getting too shiny.

11. MASCARA: Wouldn't leave home without a couple coats on my lashes. I always go for black.

12. LIP GLOSS: I usually go with something clear and moisturizing—or maybe, if I'm feeling extra-fun, something with shimmer or a slight peach hue.

Don't forget that application tips for most of these products are in chapter 6. Familiarize yourself with those before you try the tutorials, or refer back to them whenever you need to.

EVERYDAY LOOKS

If there's one thing every girl needs to know when it comes to makeup, it's how to execute a pretty, low-key, go-to look. It's a great foundation for building on your skills. To that end, I'm going to take you through my everyday makeup steps; then with Amy Nadine's help, I will expand on the theme for several different girls.

My usual look involves low-key colors and a strong eye (thanks to my liquid eyeliner). I've gotten it all down to a science and never spend more than ten minutes in front of the mirror.

TOOLS: Foundation brush, concealer brush, powder brush, angled bronzer brush, blush brush, eyebrow spoolie.

PRODUCTS: Foundation, concealer, under-eye concealer, translucent powder, bronzer, powder blush, liquid liner, mascara, lip gloss.

STEP 1: With a foundation brush or your fingers, warm up a dab of lightweight foundation in the palm of your hand.

STEP 2: Blend the foundation evenly across your entire face and neck.

STEP 3: Load up a brush with concealer in your exact shade and pat it onto any blemishes. Pat under-eye concealer (which is lighter in color than regular concealer) below your eyes. I often use a brush or sponge, but sometimes I just use my fingertips.

STEP 4: Dust translucent powder along your forehead, nose, and chin.

STEP 5: Take an angled brush, suck in your cheeks, and sweep bronzer across the hollows of your cheeks. Then dab a bit on your temples, along your hairline, and along the sides of your nose. You can also bronze under your chin.

STEP 6: Smiling at yourself in the mirror, use a blush brush to blot a coral-hued color onto the apples of your cheeks.

STEP 7: Use a spoolie brush or lash/brow comb to groom your eyebrows, brushing up and in the direction the hair grows.

STEP 8: With one motion, drag liquid liner across your upper lid, winging it out slightly at the end. If you can rest your elbow on your counter, you'll have an easier time keeping your hand steady. (See page 158 for a specific lesson on this.)

STEP 9: Apply two coats of mascara horizontally and vertically.

STEP 10: Dab on a little lip gloss and you're done!

My look can work for you even if you look nothing like me. You might be able to just follow the steps above, but if your skin tone or features are drastically different from mine, you will benefit from some of the modifications that follow.

IF YOU HAVE A MONOLID

Many Asian women (although not only Asian women) have single eyelids, which means there's no crease, and their lashes grow pretty straight. Getting flawless eyes requires a few modifications to my everyday steps.

TOOLS: Lid brush, crease brush, lash curler.

PRODUCTS: Eye shadows, eyeliner, mascara.

STEP 1: With a lid brush, sweep a light taupe shadow over the entire eye area.

STEP 2: With the same brush, sweep a medium taupe shadow from the lash line to midway up the lid.

STEP 3: With a crease brush, sweep a warm brown shadow along and just above where medium taupe stops, starting at the outer corners so that most of the color saturation is focused there.

STEP 4: Line the upper lash line with a thick dark brown or black liner and then blend it down into your lashes with your finger.

STEP 5: Use a lash curler to curl your lashes. Place the curler at the base of your lashes and squeeze gently but firmly. Hold for a few seconds, then release and inch it out, squeezing and holding a couple more times.

STEP 6: Add a coat of mascara to your top lashes only; then follow my everyday steps on page 122 for face, cheeks, and lips.

The key is to find a red-based foundation that is warm and not ashy—you don't want to look washed out and gray. Bobbi Brown and Iman make the best foundation options for dark skin. After that, the modifications for you are all about intensity.

TOOLS: Foundation brush, eye-shadow brush, powder brush.

PRODUCTS: Foundation, cream blush, eye shadow, eyeliner, mascara, powder, lip liner, lip gloss.

STEP 1: Apply foundation evenly over your entire face.

STEP 2: Smile in the mirror and, with a foundation brush, apply cream blush to the apples of your cheeks and continue back along the cheekbones.

STEP 3: Wet an eye-shadow brush and mix it with a light-colored shadow to create a paste. Apply shadow in an even layer over your entire lid. Try a light pearlized shadow with a little shimmer for daytime.

STEP 4: Apply eyeliner to the top lash line. A dark metallic color is nice.

129

STEP 5: Brush some mascara onto your top lashes only.

STEP 6: Lightly apply a layer of powder in the same shade as your foundation.

STEP 7: Define your lip line with a lip liner that is the same color as your gloss. When you're applying, make sure to follow your natural lip line. Finish with a gloss.

This look is similar to my everyday makeup routine, but the key is to define your features and avoid looking too washed out. Skip eyeliner and instead define your eyes using mascara only. Then go for a red- or pink-tinted lip balm to add a sheer but bright pop of color. Freckles are beautiful and should be shown off! Start your everyday makeup with these steps to ensure you're getting coverage but letting your freckles show through.

TOOLS: Foundation brush, concealer brush, blush brush.

PRODUCTS: Tinted moisturizer, under-eye concealer, concealer, mascara, powder blush, tinted lip balm.

STEP 1: Instead of foundation, use a small amount of tinted moisturizer—if it's still providing too much coverage, mix in a bit of untinted moisturizer to thin out the color.

STEP 2: Apply under-eye concealer. And, using a concealer brush, go back in and cover up any blemishes with concealer while steering clear of your freckles.

STEP 3: Apply mascara to your top and bottom lashes. You may want to give your lashes an extra coat if they are really light.

STEP 4: Apply a pink or peach powder blush.

STEP 5: Finish with some tinted lip balm.

READER Q: WHY DOES MY FOUNDATION TURN ORANGE?

There are ingredients in most foundation formulations that can oxidize, a process that oily skin can speed up. This is what can make your face look either orange or ashy gray. Be sure to test out products before you buy them (ask for samples or have a makeup artist apply foundation at the cosmetics counter and head to lunch before you hand over your credit card), and consider trying a shade lighter to see if it ultimately oxidizes to the right shade. Sometimes a layer of silicone-based primer before foundation can help with this too.

IF YOU HAVE STRONG FEATURES

If you are blessed with full lips or great cheekbones or big eyes, show them off! Play down the rest of your face so your best feature can shine. If you have amazing lips, for example, follow my everyday steps, but instead of liquid eyeliner, go more low-key and use a pencil. Then, instead of finishing with a gloss, choose a bolder color for your lips.

IF YOU HAVE AN OLIVE COMPLEXION

Olive skin tones are so gorgeous with warmer colors like coral on the cheeks, chocolates and bronze tones on the eyes, and a rosy or peach lip. Avoid icy colors because they will clash with your skin.

THE NO-MAKEUP MAKEUP LOOK

Sometimes you want to look healthy and refreshed, but not at all made-up. A few products and steps will get you there!

TOOLS: Foundation brush, small blush brush, eyebrow spoolie or brow brush, firm angled brush (small), concealer brush, eyelash curler, small blending brush.

PRODUCTS: Foundation, cream blush, brow powder, concealer, eyeliner, mascara, translucent powder, tinted lip balm.

STEP 1: Apply a lightweight foundation evenly over your face.

STEP 2: Blend some cream blush onto the apples of your cheeks.

STEP 3: Comb through your eyebrows with a spoolie or brow brush.

STEP 4: Using a firm angled brush and brow powder that matches the color of your brows (eye shadow works for this too), fill in your eyebrows.

STEP 5: Dab some concealer onto anything that needs concealing.

STEP 6: Using an eyeliner pencil, apply liner on your top lash line close to the water line but not actually hitting it. (Your water line is the inside of your lid.) To do this, approach from under the lashes and dab the pencil tip between the lashes.

STEP 7: Curl your lashes. Place the curler at the base of your lashes and squeeze gently but firmly. Hold for a few seconds, then release and inch it out, squeezing and holding a couple more times.

STEP 8: Apply one coat of mascara to your top lashes.

STEP 9: Translucent powder your T-zone with a small blending brush.

STEP 10: Finish with some tinted lip balm.

If you're anything like me, you tend to hit that snooze button a few times too many and often find yourself rushing to get out the door. For those all-too-frequent mornings, Amy Nadine taught me a few key shortcuts.

TOOLS: Sponge, angled bronzer brush, blush brush.

PRODUCTS: Powder foundation, bronzer, powder blush, eyeliner, mascara, lip gloss.

STEP 1: After you moisturize, instead of using foundation and concealer, apply a powder-foundation formula, which is a cream base that turns into a powder. Take a sponge and literally wipe it all over your neck and face (including your eyelids).

STEP 2: Brush bronzer below your cheekbones and along your hairline, neck, and the sides of your nose.

STEP 3: Apply blush to the apples of your cheeks.

STEP 4: Line your top eyelids with a pencil (or wet eye shadow).

STEP 5: Apply mascara to top and bottom lashes.

STEP 6: Finish with a swipe of lip gloss.

HIGHLIGHTING AND CONTOURING

Highlighting and contouring are two methods that are often skipped, but if done correctly they're pretty powerful. They can make your face look more symmetrical, both accentuate and downplay your features, and generally define and brighten your face. If you've ever taken an introductory painting class, the same principles apply here. Adding shadows makes things look farther away; adding reflective, light areas makes something look closer. Below, the images on the left show, in an exaggerated way, where you can apply each product.

CONTOURING:

This can bring out cheekbones, create a more defined chin, and streamline your nose. For subtle contouring, use bronzer; for more staying power, use a foundation that's three shades darker than your usual foundation.

HIGHLIGHTING:

This brightens up eyes (I sometimes do this instead of using under-eye concealer), makes your cheeks pop, and helps define your upper-lip area. Some highlighters add just a hint of brightness while others bring an appealing shimmer to your face.

142

TACKLING FACE ISSUES

So we all have things about our faces that we're not crazy about, whether it's a birthmark; acne scars; a nose that's too long, or too short, or too big, or too narrow; eyes that are too far apart, too close together, too small, too big. . . . Mine is how asymmetrical I am. I got a little obsessed with it, actually, when I had to look at the cover of *Lauren Conrad Style* over and over. (Go check it out if you don't believe me.)

It's totally common to fixate on a feature that seems less than desirable and decide in your mind that it's the one thing keeping you from being beautiful. But often the most beautiful faces are the ones composed of features that are the most interesting, not the most perfect. Think how boring it would be if we all looked exactly the same.

All that said, I did poll readers on what beauty issues you'd most like me to address and a lot of people wanted to learn how to finesse their so-called flaws. So on the following pages are Amy Nadine's tactics for putting your best face forward.

One Simple Thing You Can Do Every Day

Growing up, I had never heard of, and never used, exfoliator. But these days, it's one of my most trusted products. There's really nothing worse than flaky-looking foundation, so to ensure that it goes on smoothly—and stays smooth—I gently exfoliate my face a couple days a week. And the key word here is gently—don't use anything too harsh or scrub too aggressively— it takes very little to help slough off those dead skin cells! To make it extra gentle, you can mix a bit of exfoliator in with your normal cleanser.

CONCEALING A BLEMISH

If you have a whitehead, resist the urge to pop it, particularly if you're heading out the door. (For proper popping instructions, see page 28.) Instead hold a wet, hot washcloth over it for at least a minute and then gently rub off the whitehead without inflaming it. Mist your skin with toner and let your face dry. Apply foundation and then assess what needs to be covered. Using a concealer brush (go for one that's thin and pointed), dab a small amount of concealer (it should exactly match the shade of your foundation) on the blemish in quick, swirling motions. Blend away the edges with your finger and then set with powder. If you absolutely can't get enough coverage with standard makeup because you have severe or cystic acne, you can buy theatrical makeup. Just be sure to remove it fully every night!

MAKING THIN LIPS LOOK FULLER

You have to be very careful not to make your lips look visibly drawn on—or like your lipstick is spreading across your face. In general, shimmery lip gloss is going to be your best friend, since it will reflect a lot of shine and create the illusion of a bigger mouth. Look for a shimmery or pearlized gloss, and apply it on the fullest part of both your upper and bottom lip, which will be the middle of your mouth, by dabbing some in the center of your bottom lip and then pressing your lips together to get it on the upper lip.

MAKING A WIDE NOSE LOOK NARROWER

This is where correctly applied contour can be a huge help.

1. After you apply foundation, using the same brush or sponge, take a foundation that's one or two shades darker than your natural shade and apply it to the sides of your nose in a straight line, starting at each brow and continuing down each side to the tip.
2. Take a bit of highlighter and dot it down the bridge of your nose; blend with your finger.
3. Using the foundation brush (which still has foundation residue on it), blend with swirly motions until there is no perceptible line.

BRINGING FORWARD DEEP-SET EYES

You need to do an artful mix of darker shadows and highlighters to bring parts of the eye forward and set others back.

1. Apply highlighter across your entire lid.
2. Use a light shadow on the bottom part of the lid.
3. Apply darker shadow in the crease.
4. Apply translucent powder to set the color and prevent it from congregating in the crease.
5. Line your eyes and add mascara to the top lashes only—liner and mascara on the bottom lashes can make the eye appear smaller. Plus, the deeper your eyes are, the more those bottom lashes will hit your skin, so any mascara there would run.

MAKING CLOSE-SET EYES LOOK WIDER

The key here is to add emphasis to the outer corners of the eyes.

1. Cover the entire lid with light eye shadow all the way to the brow bone.
2. Add highlighter to the inner corner of your eye to brighten up the area.
3. Take a slightly deeper eye-shadow color and apply it from the middle of the eye out while blending well. (You'll want to stop short of the brow bone.)
4. Start your eyeliner from the inner corner of the eye, but keep it as thin as possible. You can slowly thicken the line as you reach the outer end of your lash line and then wing it out slightly.
5. Apply mascara, with extra emphasis on your outer lashes—in fact, pull the wand through at an outward angle to get them to fan a bit.

MAKING WIDE EYES LOOK MORE CLOSE SET

Create extra definition in the inner corners of your eyes to offset their wideness.

1. Cover the entire lid with light eye shadow, all the way to the brow bone.
2. Add highlighter to the outside half of your eye, starting directly under the brow bone and going all the way to the lash line.

I used to be really terrible about touching my eyes, particularly near the end of the day when they would get tired and dry. Not only would this invariably result in crazy raccoon eyes, but constantly rubbing your eyes can lead to wrinkles in the future. If you can't resist rubbing your eyes, or if you find that your mascara migrates down your face regardless of whether you rub your eyes or not, it might be because your mascara is drying up and needs to be replaced. If you know that eye rubbing is a habit that you just can't break, try clear mascara—it's not as potent as black, but it's better than having smudges!

3. Apply a slightly darker eye shadow in a half oval on the inner corner of your eye.
4. Keeping it nice and skinny, use liquid eyeliner across the entire upper lash line.
5. Apply a thin, two-centimeter-long strip of liquid liner starting at the inner corner of the lower lash line.

WEARING EYE MAKEUP WITH GLASSES

Contrary to what you might think—that eyeglasses are going to conceal your eye makeup—they might actually make it look more pronounced, so keep it simple but bold. Skip eye shadow and rely on a liquid liner for a heavier line, an eyelash curler (so your lashes won't hit your lenses), and a few coats of mascara.

CHAPTER EIGHT
Party Makeup

*T*here is something sort of magical about a glitzy night that calls for a beautiful face of makeup. Whether it's a dance, gala, or wedding, it's an evening that allows you to don those daring shades that rarely see the light of day. These are the evenings we can look forward to on those "left my house with wet hair and only wearing lip balm" days.

I remember being sixteen and counting the minutes until a spring formal when I could slip out of my flip-flops and into a sparkly pair of heels, have my beach-blond hair twisted into an updo and adorned with a flower (I always wore a flower in my hair when attending a dance . . . still not sure why), and apply my makeup heavily and incorporate strip lashes for drama. When I look back, my self-applied makeup didn't always look amazing, but the important thing is, in those moments, that was exactly how I felt.

Even though those steps toward growing up aren't always going to be picture-perfect, you should be fearless in experimenting with makeup. If I weren't scared of being photographed in a less-than-flattering way, I'm guessing I'd step out in questionable looks all the time—the kind of looks you can only decide were a success or a horrendous failure in retrospect. I may not leave the confines of my apartment in them, but I try out said questionable looks on nights at home when there's nowhere I need to go. It's the best way to learn. In this chapter, you'll find my favorite go-to party looks, plus a host of tips from Amy Nadine on how to adapt them to your own skin tone and features.

MY GO-TO
PARTY-MAKEUP SUPPLIES

In addition to the products I turn to as part of my everyday look (see page 118), I always have these extras on hand to prepare for an evening out:

1. KOHL EYELINER PENCIL: I blend a kohl pencil along the bottom lash line. It's smoky (i.e., sexy), and when it's dark out, I like to have a slightly more intense effect on my eyes.

2. METALLIC EYELINER: It can be really pretty to add a little steel or antique gold liner to your bottom lash line. (Pewter, navy, and deep plum metallics work too.) It won't make your eyes look smaller (which black liner can do), but it will create a little shine. If I'm feeling extra-fancy, Amy Nadine taught me to blend a pearlized nude shadow near the tear duct and at the inner corners of the bottom lash line.

3. INDIVIDUAL LASHES: A strip lash (where the lashes are all on a single strip you cut to fit your eye) is usually a bit too much for me, so I take the time to apply a few individual lashes which deliver the same fuller lashes effect in a more natural way. We'll get into the steps to this on page 155. They can be challenging to apply, so it's definitely worth experimenting with different application techniques until you get it right.

4. LASH GLUE: I always buy glue that's tinted black so that I don't have to worry about it drying clear or white. It just adds to the whole effect. Amy Nadine prefers the clear glue because it's easier to determine when it's dry. (It turns clear!) Really it just comes down to personal preference.

5. RED OR HOT PINK LIPSTICK: While I prefer a clear lip gloss or one with a subtle peach tint for daytime, at night I like to bring in satin or matte lipstick.

That said, if I go for a strong statement with my lip color, I do my liquid liner on the eye with nothing on the bottom lash line and skip false lashes.

READER Q: HOW DO I KEEP MY MAKEUP IN PLACE?

This is a common makeup question, and the truth is, it can be tough. (This is why Amy Nadine stays with me through every photo- and video-shoot, since I require constant touch-ups.) The quick answer? Powder. Translucent, pressed, or loose powder is your secret ally. If I need my makeup to stay put through an event, Amy Nadine will set my makeup at every step with a thin layer of translucent powder: after foundation and concealer, after cream blush and cream bronzer, and before she applies liner and mascara. She then sends me off with a touch-up kit for bathroom breaks. Until there's the equivalent of hair spray for your face, it's the only alternative!

For a red or vibrant lip that needs to stay in place, you'll want to color in your lips with a liner that's roughly the same shade as your lips. Then apply one coat of lipstick and blot it with a tissue. Load an eye-shadow-blending brush with loose powder and then tap it onto the entire lip area. Then go back in with another coat of lipstick. To prevent it from feathering, dab a cotton swab in powder and carefully trace the outer rim of your lip.

For eyeliner, choose a long-wear option, since they don't smudge as easily. Also, before you apply the liner, brush some powder or an eye shadow that matches your skin tone across your lid. This will help provide a good base for the liner.

PARTY LOOKS

At night, more is generally more, which can be liberating—never do I wing my liner with greater enthusiasm and confidence than when I'm heading out to an under-lit party or a candlelit dinner. That's when makeup can really create a mood as well as provide one of its most important functions: It defines our features when they'd otherwise be washed out.

This is my go-to whenever I want to look chic but not overdone. It's basically a more dramatic version of my everyday look. I always start with a clean, fresh face. Sometimes before an event, I'll get a facial or have my eyebrows done, but I never do it the day of. You should always give your skin time to calm down after any treatment.

TOOLS: Foundation brush, concealer brush, contouring brush, tweezers, lash glue, blush brush.

PRODUCTS: Foundation, concealer, bronzer, liquid eyeliner, mascara, individual lashes, blush, red lipstick.

STEP 1: Even out the face with foundation, cover any blemishes with concealer, and contour with bronzer. (See page 122 for a refresher on this process.)

STEP 2: Apply liquid liner in a classic, winged shape. (See page 158.)

STEP 3: Follow with two coats of mascara.

STEP 4: Apply seven individual lashes on the top lash line. (For a specific how-to, turn to page 155.)

STEP 5: Add peach-toned blush to the apples of the cheeks.

STEP 6: Finish with a classic red lip.

If you have dark or olive skin, it's still about the eyes. You could add a few individual lashes, you could rim your bottom water line (never use liquid eyeliner for this; choose a black kohl or kajal liner instead, and be very gentle when pulling down the lower lid and tracing the pencil back and forth), or you could try liner on both the bottom and top lash lines. Have fun with your blush too by choosing something with a little shimmer.

The key to using false lashes that look real is to go for the individuals instead of strips—and to stock up on them in all lengths (Short, Medium, Long, Mini Flare). Getting them into the right place on your lashes takes a bit of practice, but years ago Amy Nadine convinced me that I could learn how to do it, and eventually I did. The most annoying thing is when the lashes roll on their sides while the glue is drying, but trust that it happens to all of us, and don't give up! You can either use your fingers to apply them (like Amy Nadine does) or tweezers (I find that this gives me more control). Get ready by pulling out four Mediums and three Shorts and place them in separate rows on the back of your hand. This is the correct amount for one of my eyes. You may need to experiment with different lengths and combinations if you have extra-long or extra-short lashes.

STEP 1: Apply two coats of mascara to your top and bottom lashes.

STEP 2: Place a small dollop of lash glue onto the back of your hand. Let it dry for at least a minute so it gets a little tacky.

STEP 3: Start with the outside corner of one eye and place two Mediums on the very end, as close to each other as possible. You'll dip the end of each lash into the glue just before placing it. The idea is for the false lashes to blend in with your own, so place at the same angle.

STEP 4: Directly next to the two Mediums, start adding lashes, moving toward the center of your eye.

If you want to add drama to your eyes but don't think you can master individual lashes, try using strip lashes. These are great for Asian women or anyone with a monolid.

TOOLS: Eyeliner brush or pencil.

PRODUCTS: Lash glue, strip lashes, eye shadow.

STEP 1: Prep a strip of lashes by sizing it to your lash line. If it's longer, trim off the outer end. Once you're sure the size is right, glide a thin layer of lash glue across the base of the lashes.

STEP 2: Place the fake lash strip on your top lashes. It takes a few minutes for the glue to dry—you'll know it's done when the white turns clear.

TIP: If you are having difficulty placing the lashes, try using both hands.

STEP 3: Line your bottom lashes using a pencil or eye shadow and an eyeliner brush. (Approach from below the lashes.)

READER Q: HOW DO I MASTER WINGED EYELINER?

The winged look is best achieved with liquid eyeliner (although there's no rule against using a pencil for a softer result). The trick to mastering liquid eyeliner, which is standard in both my everyday and party makeup kits, is to practice a lot. If you're wary of trying it on your face, practice first on the back of your hand. Remember that the more pressure you apply, the thicker the line will be. And after you have drawn your liner on, you can either keep it as is or go back and apply more until you build it up to the thickness you desire; or you can aim for perfection and then clean up any messes afterward using a cotton swab and some makeup remover. Remember, it's all temporary so have fun, and if you make a mistake, simply remove it and start again.

If you can, rest your elbow on the bathroom counter so that you only need to move your wrist. (Trying to control your entire arm is tricky.)

It's important to note that this technique doesn't work for all eye shapes. If the skin at the outer corner of your eye is at all folded over, this look might not be for you. You can lightly tug the skin at the outer corner to draw the line at the proper angle, but it won't look exactly the same and won't look right if you try for a longer wing. Instead you should go for a subtle flick up at the end, which gives a similar effect.

STEP 1: Place the brush or pencil on your lash line at the inner corner of your eye, and keeping the line against your lashes, drag it outward, stopping at the outer corner of your eye. Start small. (You can always retrace your step to make the line thicker.)

STEP 2: Now wing the liner out. Imagine a line going from the outside corner of your eye, up to about where your brow ends—that's the angle you're following. I stop where my eye crease ends (about the length of an eyelash), but you can inch it out incrementally until you find the perfect cat-eye for you. Sometimes just a little is all you need.

STEP 3: Go back and fill in the wing, connecting the two lines you've created and thickening the curve.

STEP 4: Once you have a smooth line, clean up any other imperfections with a cotton swab and you're done!

THE SUBTLE SMOKY EYE

This is a traditional smoky eye, but to make it more subtle, Amy Nadine uses coppers, fawns, golds, and chocolates instead of a standard gray palette. The key to getting this right is to blend the eye shadow really well. And don't be afraid of messing up (that's what cotton swabs and makeup remover are for)—in fact, it's supposed to be a little messy.

TOOLS: Flat eye-shadow brush, crease brush, blending brush, angled brush.

PRODUCTS: Various eye shadows, eyeliner, mascara.

STEP 1: Apply a fawn color all over the entire lid with a lay-down brush (a flat eye-shadow brush).

STEP 2: Using a crease brush, apply copper in the crease and then, with a clean blending brush, blend by using the brush like a windshield wiper.

STEP 3: With an angled brush, sweep a metallic chocolate shade along your lower lash line. (You can also add a nude color to the brow bone and near the tear duct.)

STEP 4: Coat the lower water line with a dark brown kajal liner or shadow.

STEP 5: Apply two coats of mascara.

One Simple Thing You Can Do Every Day

Everyone always focuses on putting *on* makeup, but try never to skip the important step of taking it off. It can be all too tempting after a long, fun night out to collapse into bed with a full face of makeup. (I have even invested in fancy white pillowcases to discourage the practice.) Even though it's the last thing you want to do, it's really important to take five minutes to remove your eye makeup and fully wash your face. To expedite the process if you wear a lot of foundation, it could be worth investing in something like a Clarisonic brush. If you do tend to fall asleep with makeup on, be sure to wash your pillowcases often.

If you're heading for a night out directly after work or school, you can go right in for some strategic touch-ups rather than having to start fresh again. Since I often find myself at my office or in a late meeting until the last second—and unable to return home before dinner or a party—I've learned to stash mini kits of the below products everywhere: in my car, in a handful of my most-used purses, and in my office.

TOOLS: Sponge, cotton swabs, lay-down eye-shadow brush, blush brush.

PRODUCTS: Hydrating mist, powder foundation, eye-makeup remover, metallic eye shadow, eyeliner, blush, mascara, lip gloss.

STEP 1: If your face is looking a bit cakey, mist it with a hydrating/refresher mist (i.e., nothing too astringent).

STEP 2: Using a sponge, smooth out any spots where the makeup has creased in the lines on your face. If your foundation has vanished completely, take a sponge and smooth on a powder-foundation formula. (It turns to powder once it's on your skin.)

STEP 3: Blend any eye makeup that's creased in your lid crease with your ring finger.

STEP 4: Take a little bit of eye-makeup remover on a cotton swab and clean up your under-eye area, since your eye makeup most likely shifted down over the course of the day.

STEP 5: Using a lay-down brush, apply a metallic wet shadow to your entire lid. You're wetting it for more intensity.

STEP 6: Redo your eyeliner, thickening it a bit.

STEP 7: Reapply blush (and bronzer, if that's part of your regular makeup). If you're going out somewhere fancy, you'll want to use a slightly heavier hand than you did in the morning.

STEP 8: Put on a fresh coat of mascara.

STEP 9: Finish with some lip gloss.

Lesson Learned

This is usually a lesson learned in retrospect, but try to pick only one feature to highlight—even after 9:00 p.m. If you prefer a dramatic, smoky eye, then balance it out with a neutral lip. If you're going to do a pop of color on your cheeks, skip any eye shadow that's going to battle it. If you like a red lip, go easy on everything else. It's great to have fun, but you don't want to look like a clown!

CHAPTER NINE
Everyday Hair

*H*air can be a quick visual indicator of what sort of person you are, maybe even more so than the clothes you choose to wear. Is your hair short and pixieish? Long and beachy? Huge and untamed? Do you spend an hour on it every morning or walk out of the house with it wet and let whatever happens happen? The answer says a lot about you. That's probably why a bad-hair day can be much more stressful than any outfit indecision.

Over the last few years, my basic hairstyle has remained pretty much the same. I've played around a little with the color and length but I have always returned to my blond waves. This is partly because I've made some bad decisions on both counts, and I don't want to relive those recovery days. (I had to wear extensions for years while my hair slowly grew out from a bad cut.) It's also because I know what works best for me now. Plus, it's fun to try all sorts of updos and braids when I'm eager to switch up my general silhouette.

A big part of great everyday hair is finding the right tools for your hair type. So here is some information about basic hair tools and some lessons on technique.

PRODUCTS

There are as many hairstyling products as there are types of hair, and finding the right combination for you depends on a lot of different factors—not just your hair type but the style you're going for, the tools you plan to use, where you live (because both climate and the type of water in your city's supply can have an impact on your hair), how often you style your hair, and so on. So you'll have to do some experimenting on your own. But here are some tips to keep in mind:

- Always use some kind of heat-protecting product when you're blowing out, curling, or straightening your hair.

- If you have fine, thin hair and are looking to pump up the volume, there are a lot of great volumizers and thickeners on the market. But avoid ones that rely on copolymers. This is the ingredient in hair products that helps with hold by making the strands stick together. (The technical name is PVP/VA copolymer.) It works by preventing each strand from absorbing moisture and only lasts for a short period because it breaks down easily. Your hair will look great . . . until a couple hours after you've applied the product.

- If you have curls that tend to get big and frizzy, applying leave-in conditioner to your hair while it's wet is a great option.

- If you have short hair, always keep it nicely trimmed to maintain the shape and know your texture when choosing products. Long hair is more forgiving when it comes to hair products—with short hair, the wrong product will be much more noticeable. Your stylist is a great resource, so be sure to ask him or her for recommendations when you're getting those regular trims.

- For color-treated hair, avoid products with too much alcohol because it dries the strands and leaches out the color.

- A soft-hold mousse is a great choice if you have curls or waves you're trying to tame.

- Your best product might be a combination of several. Leave-in conditioner plus mousse while your hair is wet, then a little serum or hair spray when it's dry. Experiment to find your perfect product cocktail!

- For everyday use, go easy on the hair spray—a light- or medium-hold formula will do.

- Know your hair, because understanding the type, texture, and density of your locks will help guide you to products best suited for you. (Turn to page 47 for a refresher.)

TOOLS

Unlike with makeup, where you can accumulate a drawer full of brushes and other tools to help you achieve your look, for hair it's all about what works best for your hair type and what style you're going for. Everyone should have a great brush, but beyond that, it depends on your everyday process.

An Encyclopedia of Brushes

There are a lot of fancy, specialized brushes out there (most of which have been in production for ages)—in many different shapes. It can be hard to figure out which is most appropriate for your hair. I use a round thermal brush when I'm blowing out my hair and a paddle brush when I'm combing it smooth. But Kristin uses all kinds depending on what type of hair she's working with.

THE PADDLE BRUSH

This is a serious multitasker (and must-have). It's great for detangling hair and ensuring that you get a smooth blowout. If you like to add volume to your crown, this is perfect for that. Choose a brush that has perfectly rounded nylon pin bristles, because those won't scratch your scalp. (They will actually massage it.)

THE BRISTLED ROUND BRUSH

This is another multitasker and is key for adding waves to any blowout. It holds the hair with the perfect amount of tension (without creating tangles) and adds bounce and shine.

THE METAL ROUND BRUSH

This brush is vented, which means that air can pass through (and dry the strands from all angles), and because the barrel is metal, it acts like a curling iron when your hair dryer heats it up. You should use this only if you're speedy with a blowout though. You can end up creating too much heat, and the bristles can scratch your scalp if you're not careful.

THE BOAR- AND NYLON-BRISTLED METAL BRUSH

Sounds pretty specific, right? It's actually super-versatile, since it's a combo deal, which gives you more control without the danger of generating too much heat. Boar bristles are good for creating tension, so if you have curly hair this is a great choice for a brush to use for a blowout. Alternatively, if you have thick, straight hair and want to add curl, this brush is good for that.

THE SMALL BOAR-BRISTLED BRUSH

This brush is ideal for bangs, particularly unruly bangs. Because it is small, you can get close to the forehead, avoiding the dreaded ski-jump bangs effect.

THE BOAR-BRISTLED OVAL-CUSHIONED BRUSH

I use this brush for everything, including smoothing down flyaways, brushing out curls, and soft teasing. The Mason Pearson is the Rolls-Royce of boar-bristled brushes, and it isn't cheap. If you can swing it though, it's worth it.

How to Find the Right Hair Dryer

You've probably been using the same hair dryer forever, which is totally fine—for the most part, the mechanics of hair dryers haven't changed much over the years, besides becoming a bit more powerful. The important thing is to be sure that you have the right pieces to affix to the end. For a blowout, you absolutely need a nozzle to direct the stream of air. If you're trying to dry your hair yet keep curl, then you need to attach a diffuser to keep your hair from becoming too frizzy.

If you're looking to invest in a new hair dryer, there are a couple things to keep in mind. One of the most important factors is weight. If you're going to be holding a hair dryer over your head while mastering a blowout, you need to do whatever you can to prevent arm fatigue—and here, extra ounces can really add up. Kristin gave me an Elchim 2001, which I use every day. It's lightweight, powerful, and gets nice and hot. If you're not particularly fast with a blow-dryer and you need to go over your strands again and again, you want a dryer that sends out more air and a little less heat, like the Solano.

How to Find the Right Straightening Iron

If you've seen *Hairspray*, you're probably well-versed in the fact that our mothers and grandmothers used actual irons to straighten their hair. Not the safest approach, but snaps to them for creativity! These days though, you can just invest in one of the many flatirons that are specially formulated for hair.

If you have very curly hair that you straighten frequently, you need a high-quality iron to limit the amount of damage you're doing to your hair. A lot of people like ceramic irons, but if you think about it, ceramic is clay, which by nature absorbs moisture. I feel that it's too drying for my hair over time, so I use an iron that's made of metal. If you only use this tool occasionally, and only for minor repair work or your bangs, you don't need to buy a top-of-the-line iron—but you should look for a model that heats up quickly, to save you time.

If you have fine or colored hair—i.e., hair that's easily damaged—look for an iron with a wide range of heat settings (there are some variations that let you set a precise temperature). When you're working on your hair, pay attention to the number of times you need to move the iron through your hair to get the results you need. If you're passing the iron over the strands more than twice, invest in one that gets hotter. It's better to

One Simple Thing You Can Do Every Day

As you might remember from chapter 3, the more you style your hair with heat tools, the more likely you are to damage the strands. Because I rely pretty heavily on blowouts and have my hair styled constantly, I try to extend times between shampoos as much as possible to limit the amount of blowouts I have to do from start to finish. And when I do shampoo my hair, I condition it extensively. I always try to leave enough time to allow for a good five-minute leave-in conditioner for the bottom two-thirds of my hair. I'll apply it, comb it through all of my strands with a wide-tooth comb, and then let it soak in and permeate all the cuticles for as long as I can stand to wait it out in the shower.

And whenever possible, I let my hair air-dry, just to give it a break. This is a good solution on weekends when I'm not working. Seems like my hair deserves a break from the work every once in a while too!

get it in one pass with slightly more, evenly distributed heat, than to have to go over it repeatedly. In general, if you have thicker hair, you should set your iron at 400–420°F. If your hair is finer, go for 280–350°F.

How to Select the Right Size Curling Iron

When you're shopping for a curling iron, the same general rules apply as with a flatiron. You want a curling iron that holds consistent heat, particularly if you tend to curl your entire head of hair. Most models set heat on a scale of 1–10. If you have thicker hair, aim for 8–10; if you have finer hair, aim for 5–7.

You'll want to choose a curling-iron barrel that matches the size of the curl you'd like to make—i.e., smaller curls or beachier waves? Some styles look best with varying sizes of curls, so they require more than one iron. Unless you're quite skilled, you might also want to try a curling wand, since it's hard to avoid leaving clip marks in your curls (if you pay attention at your salon, you'll notice that your stylist either uses a wand or has permanently fastened the clamp down). While it is designed to keep the hair in place, that little clamp is usually more trouble than it's worth. But all that aside, here's a breakdown on the size of the barrel and what it will do for your hair.

$^3/_8$ INCH AND $^5/_8$ INCH: If you have naturally tight curls and only need an iron to refine them to avoid frizziness, one of these is your new best friend.

$^3/_4$ INCH: This iron's not too wide and won't result in overly ringlet-y hair, but the curls will still be tight.

1 INCH: This is good for creating larger curls and waves—unless your hair is inclined to hold curl and can handle something bigger, this is your go-to if you want a beachier head of hair. (This is the size I typically use.)

2 INCH: For voluminous curls and for creating general volume, this is the perfect size.

EVERYDAY LOOKS

When my hair is at its most basic, i.e., mornings when I'm just heading straight to the office, I like a nice blowout with subtle waves. I've learned a lot from Kristin Ess, so I've gotten pretty good at executing a blowout on myself, but I know it's not easy if you haven't mastered it. Don't give up! It takes time but eventually it will just click, and you'll figure out how to hold your wrist correctly and how to use the dryer in the right way for your hair type.

MY EVERYDAY WAVES

Even though I have a blowout down to a relative science, the results vary. But it doesn't matter since I always go back in with a curling iron to add waves. The blowout is just a means to an end—you always want your hair to be dry when you take an iron to it.

STEP 1: Apply a heat-protecting serum to the ends of your hair and start blow-drying. Make sure you dry problem areas first. (I have a cowlick so I always blow out this section before it has time to dry on its own.)

STEP 2: Separate your hair into three sections: two on either side of your neck, and one on the top of your head. I start on the right side of my neck, and I pin up the top section to keep it out of my way.

STEP 3: Take a 1" curling iron and, starting halfway to three-quarters up each strand of hair, put the hair inside the clamp and wrap the remaining hair around the barrel.

STEP 4: After releasing each curl, comb through it to soften it a bit.

STEP 5: After finishing the first half of your hair, comb the entire side to find a pattern. Repeat the same steps on the other side.

STEP 6: Put a little dab of silicon-based serum in your palm, warm it up, and apply to the ends.

STEP 7: Mist your whole head with a light hair spray. You want the curls to remain soft, so don't overspray.

On the following pages, you'll find a few more everyday looks for you to try out!

PINNED BACK

I love wearing my hair down, but don't always love having to push it out of my face. This look is the perfect solution.

STEP 1: Tease a small section at the back of your head. (This is what you're going to anchor your other pieces to with bobby pins.)

STEP 2: If you want to pin it back on both sides, part your hair in the middle. (You can also pin back on just one side.)

STEP 3: Take a section from the side, near the front hairline. Twist the piece back and then tease the hair about three-quarters of the way down.

STEP 4: Take the teased part of the strand and connect it with the teased section on your crown. Anchor it with a bobby pin.

STEP 5: Repeat on the other side.

MESSY BUN

This look is great for those mornings when you don't feel like messing around to make your long hair look right.

 STEP 1: Gather your hair into a high ponytail on the top of your head.

 STEP 2: Using a comb, tease the ponytail, adding volume—the messier the better.

 STEP 3: Wrap the hair around itself, starting in the back so the thickest part is in front. Depending on the length of your hair, you may have to twist it around more than once.

 STEP 4: Hold on to the end of the ponytail and pin it at the base of the bun.

STEP 5: Finish with a light mist of hair spray.

TIPS: Spray hair spray on your hand or a toothbrush for smoothing any wisps on the side. If you want it messier, you can widen the bun by pulling it apart.

GREAT CURLS

If you've got unruly hair and tend to give up and throw it in a bun or ponytail because it's looking frizzy, this technique is for you. There's no reason you can't wear your long locks down with your curls looking healthy and defined.

STEP 1: Starting with damp hair you have combed out in the shower, clip the majority of your hair on your head, leaving a small section loose at the back.

STEP 2: Apply curl cream to two sections of the back of your hair at a time.

STEP 3: Split each section into two smaller ones, twist each of those sections (twist both in the same direction) and then wrap one around the other all the way from your roots to your ends. Repeat on the other section.

STEP 4: Repeat applying cream and twisting, section by section, to finish the back of your head.

STEP 5: Move on to the sides, then complete the top and front of your hair.

STEP 6: Either diffuse your hair with a blow-dryer or buy a dryer bonnet (pictured here), which Kristin says is the best thing for girls with curls. Looks crazy, but it isn't too pricey and will control your curls.

STEP 7: Once your hair is almost dry, carefully unwrap the twisted sections. For each, start at the bottom and work your way up to the root.

STEP 8: Flip your head upside down and diffuse your curls using a hair dryer.

If your curls tend to go more toward wavy and you want to amp up the curl factor, invest in a diffuser.

STEP 1: Start with wet hair that you've combed out in the shower. Find your part.

STEP 2: Apply curl cream to your hair, starting at the roots and working down to the ends.

STEP 3: Divide your hair into thick sections and twist each one.

STEP 4: Scrunch the moisture out of your hair.

TIP: Use a T-shirt instead of a towel for less frizz.

STEP 5: Use a diffuser on the ends of your hair.

STEP 6: If you want extra volume, you can also diffuse at the root.

STEP 7: To get more defined curls, use a curling iron on several sections of your hair ($^3/_4$-inch to 1-inch). Wrap the hair around the whole barrel instead of putting it through the clamp.

HAIR
ACCESSORIES 101

I'm pretty thrilled with the resurgence of hair accessories as of late—I love their vintage vibe, and they're great tools for those days when your hair just won't do what you want it to (and also when you're trying to conceal your roots—hello, scarf!). These are the two accessories I rely on with the most frequency:

BARRETTES: I use these in a classic, old-school style. I either pin small sections of hair back on both sides of my head, or if the barrette is wide enough to accommodate a bit more hair, I pull my hair back evenly on both sides and clip the barrette at the occipital bone for a low ponytail. Sometimes I'll go all arts and crafts on my barrettes and glue bows or costume jewelry onto them.

HEADBAND: Whether it's tortoiseshell or covered in polka dots, there's a headband to match every style sensibility—I have dozens of them. Headbands are great on those days when I don't have time to style my hair or when my roots are showing more than I'd like. The key is to keep it forward on your head. Make sure there's only about an inch and a half of hair separating the front of the band from your hairline.

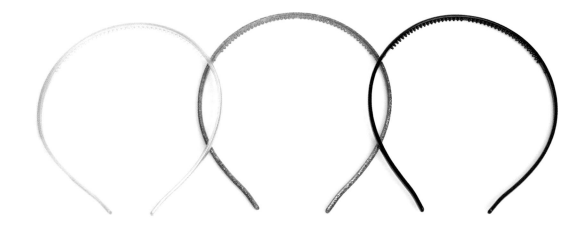

I never understood why I should only curl and straighten my hair when it is completely dry. It turns out that when you use any sort of iron directly on the cuticle while it's still wet, you're essentially steaming the strand of hair. Instant damage. Sometimes it's easy to confuse hot air with dry hair, so after you use your blow-dryer, let your head cool down for a bit to ensure that every strand is completely dry. Best-case scenario: Dry your hair, get dressed, do your makeup, and then go back in with the iron.

BRAIDS

I've never met a braid that I didn't want to try. The following pages are filled with the ones that most often appear in my hair: the classic, French, rope, fishtail, goddess, and waterfall. These are great for ho-hum hair days, special occasions, or just when you're feeling like you want to try something new! The classic and French are always great stand-bys. The rope is more interesting than a straightforward ponytail. The fishtail is beachy and, therefore, perfect for summer. (I like to wear mine down the side sometimes.) The goddess is my go-to when I want to add a little something extra to my hair but don't have the time to do anything overly complicated. The waterfall is a more delicate, complex version of the goddess that takes some practice to perfect, but I love the way it looks.

CLASSIC BRAID

STEP 1: Divide your hair into three even sections at the back of your head.

STEP 2: Cross the right section over the center, then repeat with the left.

STEP 3: Repeat until all of your hair is braided.

STEP 4: Secure the end with an elastic.

FRENCH BRAID

STEP 1: Starting at the front of your head, take a V-shaped section of hair.

STEP 2: Begin braiding, crossing the right section over the center and then repeating with the left.

STEP 3: Now repeat, but this time taking a small section of hair from either side of your head each time.

STEP 4: Once you've traveled down your entire head, braid the remaining hair.

STEP 5: Secure the end with an elastic.

ROPE BRAID

STEP 1: Pull your hair back into a ponytail and secure it with an elastic.

STEP 2: Divide your hair into two sections.

STEP 3: Twist each section. The key is to twist both sections in the same direction.

STEP 4: Wrap the two sections around each other, in the opposite direction you twisted. (So, if you twisted each strand to the right, wrap around each other to the left.) You will probably have to keep twisting as you work your way down each section, twisting as you wrap.

STEP 5: Secure the end with an elastic.

STEP 1: Divide your hair into two sections, right down the center of your head.

STEP 2: Hold the left section in your hand and take a small piece from the far outside of the right section, crossing it over to the inside of the left section.

STEP 3: Switch hands, and repeat the process for the opposite side.

STEP 4: Keep going until you've run out of hair. The key to getting the right look is to take very small pieces of hair each time.

STEP 5: Secure the end with an elastic; spray with hair spray.

STEP 6: Then go back in and loosen it up with your hands so that it's nice and messy in parts. I also tend to tug mine over to one side.

GODDESS BRAID

STEP 1: Gather a one- to two-inch section of hair in the front on one side of your head.

STEP 2: Braid to the point where you plan to pin it.

STEP 3: Secure it to the back of your head with a bobby pin that matches your hair color.

STEP 4: Spray with light-hold hair spray.

WATERFALL

STEP 1: Gather a one- to two-inch section of hair in the front of one side of your head.

STEP 2: Divide the hair into three pieces, as if you're starting a regular side braid.

STEP 3: Begin the braid, but once you've completed one regular braid cycle, drop the top piece (the closest to the front) over and through the other two sections and pull it down gently.

STEP 4: Twist the two pieces you're left with upward.

STEP 5: Grab a small section of hair and add it as the new third piece in between the two you are holding. Make sure to drop it through from the top and pull it down. The pieces you're dropping through are what form the "waterfall."

STEP 6: Twist the original two pieces again and add a new third piece. Repeat until your braid is long enough to pin back. Note: The two pieces that you're twisting are the same two pieces for the whole braid.

STEP 7: Secure it with a clear elastic and affix it to your head with a bobby pin.

CHAPTER TEN
Party Hair

*L*ike putting together a great outfit, good party hair—hair that's going to last all night—requires a strong foundation. When I'm planning an outfit for an evening out, I usually pick one focal point and build the look around it: Is it going to be a little black cocktail dress that I'll accessorize with costume jewelry and a fun shoe? Is it going to be a vintage top that I'll pair with jeans, a neutral heel, and delicate necklaces? Or maybe it's going to be a glittery miniskirt, a chiffon top, and some sky-high platforms. Whatever look I land on, my hair is an essential part of the equation. Just like with makeup, I never want to look too "done" or end up with what I refer to as "bad prom hair." You know the kind I'm talking about: when hair is so shellacked and "perfect" that it just looks kind of dorky. There are definitely moments for hair that's sleek and well-maintained, but some of my favorite 'dos are a bit more undone. They may take a good thirty minutes to construct, but they look more like they took two minutes . . . in the best possible way. It makes your beauty appear more effortless—a more casual glamour.

While there aren't any hard-and-fast rules about coordinating hair and outfits, I do try to match the two in sensibility—without taking it into costume-y territory. I probably wouldn't match a maxi dress from the '70s with Farrah Fawcett–worthy, feathered hair. If my outfit feels feminine and has a vintage vibe, I'll wear my hair down and wavy and maybe work in a braid. If my outfit feels a bit more classic, I'll wear my hair sleek or in an updo (depending on whether it's casual or more formal), and if my outfit is a bit tougher, I'll go for a high, clean ponytail or a messy bun. The right hairstyle is all in the balance, and

205

One Simple Thing You Can Do Every Day

If your daily and special-event hairstyles require a lot of product, be sure to give your hair an occasional break. I will put on a hair mask for ten minutes or, if it's coconut oil, overnight (see page 41 for recipes), use a heavy leave-in conditioner, or work in a clarifying shampoo. Hair spray, mousse, and even some shampoos and conditioners leave residue on the strand that can build up over time and alter the hair's texture, making it hard to style. It can also make your hair look dull. Clarifying shampoos are intense though, so don't use them too frequently—they can dry out your hair and strip color. (And definitely focus them on your scalp and roots, not the ends of your hair, which might already be fragile.)

as everyone knows, partly dependent on what your hair feels like doing that day! In this chapter, you'll find a few of my favorite go-tos as well as some good options for other types of hair.

TOOLS

I may have a drawer full of brushes, pins, curlers, headbands, barrettes, bows, products, etc., but you really don't need more than a few tools to execute great party hair.

MY GO-TO PRODUCTS/HAIR TOOLS/ACCESSORIES

- 1" curling iron for curls or 1¼" iron for waves
- Leave-in detangling conditioner
- Argan oil for heat protection and shine
- Strong bobby pins in my hair color
- Small clear elastics (because I wear a lot of braids)
- A flat brush
- A comb to soften curls

DIY GLAM ACCESSORIES

I'm often turning to a head scarf or a headband or a great clip to finish out a look (or to get me through a rough hair day). There are lots of affordable hair-accessory options out there at stores like Forever 21, H&M, and Kohl's, but I enjoy making my own too. Here are a few quick tricks:

TURN A VINTAGE BROOCH INTO A HAIR CLIP

I love shopping at flea markets—and I always find myself gravitating toward cool pieces of costume jewelry that I generally don't ever end up wearing as intended. But big pins can easily be transformed into good hair accessories. All you need is a metal barrette or a plastic hair comb from a drugstore or craft shop. You also need some fine wire used for beading necklaces and some glue that adheres to metal.

1. Apply a thin strip of glue along the back of the brooch in the path of where the pin and the barrette or clip will connect. Before you put the two together, let the glue dry for about thirty seconds to a minute so that it gets tacky. (And be sure to avoid getting any on your fingers!) Push the pin and the barrette or clip together and hold them until the glue is dry.
2. Next use the wire to further secure the clip to the barrette, being careful not to make it visible.

GLAMIFY A HEADBAND

Whether you wrap them entirely in ribbon, weave in some silk flowers, or add big, glittery rhinestones, headbands are like a blank canvas. All you need are some plastic headbands, the materials of your choice from the craft store, and a hot-glue gun.

BEJEWEL BARRETTES

If you have fine hair (or not a lot of hair) and are looking for a less intense hair accessory, you can bejewel small barrettes—or even bobby pins—with small strips of rhinestones or beads from the craft store. Again, all you need is a hot-glue gun or superglue and a bit of wire.

GREAT HAIR ALL NIGHT

Gravity has a way of sucking the life out of hair. And if your hair isn't incrementally flattening, there's a good chance that humidity is making it grow . . . with frizz. If only we could freeze-frame our hair as we step out of the salon. There are definitely a few things that you can do to combat these outside factors, but it's wise to keep in mind what your night might have in store as you figure out how best to style your hair. If you're at the beach, don't try to make your hair stick-straight with a straightening iron. If you're heading to a dance party, skip the sculptural up-do. Here are a few other things you can do to give your hair a fighting chance of surviving the night—without turning it into a helmet with hair spray.

- To prep a look, start with a minimal amount of product. In fact, it's best to skip it unless you absolutely need it. Sometimes, when you're dancing around, products can end up working against you. Ideally you want your hair to be pretty clean.

- As you're blowing out your hair, flip your head upside down to blast some volume into your roots. If the look involves curls, try pinning them up with setting clips until they cool, since they'll naturally loosen and come undone as the night goes on.

- Use hair spray, but don't go too crazy. Finish your look with a small amount of medium-hold hair spray. You'd be surprised at how often overspraying can ruin your look more than dancing can. Keep it light so that as you move around, your hair loosens up; eventually the hair spray will dissolve and your strands will be free to move.

- I always carry some extra bobby pins in my bag—and U-shaped pins to fix any strands that come undone from an updo. I also carry a small hand mirror so I can check the back of my hair when I'm in the restroom.

PARTY LOOKS

I love looking effortlessly put-together, so when I'm getting ready to go out, I gravitate toward hairstyles that are somewhat relaxed and lower maintenance. After all, between hourly lipstick touch-ups and deciding how much your Spanx will permit you to eat, you don't want to be worrying about your hair too.

I love this because it's simple and easy to maintain but casually elegant. Also it only takes a few minutes to do.

STEP 1: Starting with clean, dry hair, take a 1" curling iron and curl sections at random. Just be sure to curl away from the face consistently.

STEP 2: Take a dollop of water-based pomade in your palms and then rub them together to warm it up. Scrunch it into the ends of your hair to mess it up a bit.

STEP 3: Gather your hair into a high ponytail and secure it with a small, clear elastic. It doesn't have to be perfect. This style looks good with a little added texture.

STEP 4: Take a strand from the bottom of the ponytail and wrap it around the elastic to conceal it, then pin the end in with a bobby pin that's the same color as your hair.

MAKING CURLS LAST

If your hair is anything like mine, it has difficulty holding curls throughout an entire evening. A trick that I've learned is to set my curls to extend their staying power. I started doing this a couple of years ago, and it has made a big difference—I wear my hair down for events more often than I used to.

STEP 1: Divide your hair into several sections, focusing on one at a time. Pin up any sections you're not working on that might be in the way.

STEP 2: With the curling iron open, wrap a piece of hair around it (it's easier than trying to roll it up without crimping the end). Hold the clamp down for about five seconds. Depending on the barrel width, you'll get different types of curls (see page 176). I like a 1" to 1¼" curl, because I don't want ringlet-y hair, and any curl much bigger than that falls out of my hair. Another option is to toss in some hot rollers at random.

STEP 3: Release the curl and wrap it around your fingers, maintaining the shape.

STEP 4: Keeping it coiled, pin the curl to your head to set.

213

STEP 5: Once the entire head is done, mist it with hair spray.

STEP 6: After at least ten minutes (I like to let my hair set while I do my makeup), carefully unpin your curls, letting them fall gently.

STEP 7: Gently comb the curls to blend them together.

HIGH, SLEEK PONYTAIL

It can take work to get your hair sleek, but this chic look is worth the effort. It's a great look for day or night.

STEP 1: Start with straight hair—you may need to use a straightening iron to achieve this. If so, don't forget to use heat-protecting spray first.

STEP 2: Put a small amount of styling wax or pomade in the palm of your hand, rub your hands together, and then massage it into your roots for more hold.

STEP 3: Using a boar-bristle brush, gather your hair at the occipital bone, which is the highest point on the back of your head before it begins to slope down. Smooth all of the hair into your hand and secure the ponytail with a clear elastic.

STEP 4: Take a thin section of hair from the bottom of the ponytail and wrap it around the elastic.

STEP 5: Affix the end of the strand with a bobby pin (ideally one that is the same shade as your hair).

STEP 6: Spray some hair spray onto a boar-bristle brush and smooth down any flyaways for a sleeker look.

CURLING WITH A WAND

A curling wand is a great option for anyone who has difficulty using a curling iron with a clamp, and it is great for achieving that perfect party curl.

STEP 1: Start with your natural hair texture. (Your hair should be completely dry.) If you have wavy hair, the natural curl will support the curls you're adding. Pin all of your hair up on one side except the piece you're going to curl. Your piece should be the same width as the barrel of your wand. (If your wand has a 1" barrel, your piece should be an inch wide.)

STEP 2: Twist the strip around the wand and hold it for about five seconds or until the piece of hair feels heated through.

STEP 3: Slide the wand out. (Don't unravel the hair.)

STEP 4: Spray the curl immediately after you've released it from the wand.

STEP 5: Repeat on the rest of your hair.

STEP 6: Release the curls, with your fingers at your roots.

STEP 7: For a fun extra, pin your hair back on one side with a pretty clip.

STEP 8: Spray lightly with hair spray.

Retro Curl

This look has a glamorous '40s vibe and works for any hair that's longer than chin length. You'll just have fewer curls if your hair is shorter.

STEP 1: Start with clean, dry, tangle-free, freshly brushed hair.

STEP 2: Section hair into 1" to 1½" sections.

STEP 3: Take a 1" curling iron and curl hair away from the face.

STEP 4: When you release the curl, gather it gently together and pin it into place with a setting clip.

STEP 5: As you go, make sure that all the curls are placed immediately next to each other in a horizontal row.

STEP 6: When you go one row down, you'll want to stagger them, so that you're creating a checkerboard or bricklike effect. This creates the curl pattern, so it's essential. Spray with hair spray.

STEP 7: Once the curls are set, release them.

STEP 8: Comb out the curls with a flat brush to find the pattern, then spray with hair spray. If necessary, you can take a curling iron and go back in to curl the ends under.

CHAPTER ELEVEN
Nails

*L*ike my first love, I will never forget my first manicure. I was in the sixth grade and about to attend my very first school dance. I arrived at the small salon with my best friend and was greeted by a wall displaying what seemed like every shade imaginable, all contained in tiny glass bottles that lined the Lucite shelves. I admired the beautiful colors, although they served me little purpose because I already knew what I wanted: a French manicure. I couldn't imagine anything more grown-up or sophisticated than leaving that salon with my nails each lined with a hand-painted ivory tip. I remember being so cautious in the following days until that heartbreaking but inevitable first chip occurred. Nowadays I still have the same love for a beautiful manicure, but my experience is quite different. I learned quickly that frequent visits to the nail salon can become costly, and while I was existing solely on paychecks from my minimum-wage-earning retail job it simply wasn't an option. So I started to paint my own nails—and to get creative about it.

Today there are few things that give me more pleasure than coming home from a long day, spreading out my nail tools and polish, and giving myself a fresh manicure. There is something therapeutic about the whole process, and as someone who loves to constantly update my nail color, it's convenient. And it isn't only about Ferrari red and ballet-slipper pinks anymore. With the recent upswing in creative nail art, a manicure is considered more of an accessory these days. So break out that polish and have some fun with it.

CARING FOR YOUR NAILS

If you really think about it, nails are pretty weird. They're essentially talons—ones that happen to be good for peeling off stickers and slicing tape seals. While we probably have them for biological reasons, nails also serve as the perfect little canvas for expressing your personality. But before we get to the fun stuff, I want to outline some basic guidelines for nail care, so you can keep yours nice and healthy.

- Don't bite your nails. This one is a given.

- Keep your nails at a reasonable length by trimming them frequently. You don't need daggers. (In this digital age, how do you text?) This way, you'll be much less likely to break them. When it comes to trimming your toenails (which don't grow as fast as your fingernails), make sure that you cut them straight across; otherwise they can grow to the side and create ingrown toenails (ouch!).

- Speaking of toenails, it's important to keep them trimmed and to make sure that your shoes aren't too tight; otherwise you can blacken your toenails, particularly if you're a runner. Know what's not fun? Waiting for a blackened toenail to grow out. (It can take a year.)

- When you're getting a manicure or pedicure, be sure to choose a salon that properly sterilizes their tools and maintains a generally high level of cleanliness. Fungal infections are very contagious, and there's nothing worse than getting one. (As with a blackened toenail, you need to cure the fungus and then wait for the discolored nail to completely grow out, an annoyingly slow process.)

- Give your nails a breather. Putting on and removing nail polish too often can strip your nails (mostly because nail-polish remover can be harsh), so go polish-free every once in a while.

- If you get a painful hangnail, don't rip it: You'll just tear live skin. Instead gently trim it back. It will help if you do this after you take a shower.

- Keep your nails nice and moisturized. This goes a long way in the battle against brittleness. Keeping your hands clean is important, but try not to wash them excessively (and use lotion when you do, making sure to rub it into your cuticles).

- As hard as it is to resist, don't pick or peel your nail polish. Along with the color, you could be removing the top layer of your nail. Plus it just looks sloppy.

- There's nothing you can eat that will definitely improve the health of your nails (although a good diet can't hurt), but biotin supplements (part of the B-vitamin family) have been shown to help strengthen nails. As always, talk to your doctor about taking supplements.

How to Make Your Manicure Last

There's nothing more irritating than painting your nails only to chip your manicure hours later. So here are a few things to keep in mind:

• Even if you like to soak your nails (particularly before pushing back your cuticles), only paint them when they're thoroughly dry (not towel-dry). I do all my basic prep work and then wait for at least ten minutes. If the nail plate is wet, it will tighten under the polish eventually and warp the smooth surface.

• Apply thin coats. And only two if you absolutely must to make the color even. The thicker the job, the more likely it is to peel right off.

• Wait at least five minutes between coats. Time-consuming, sure, but it will help your handiwork last longer.

• It may seem old-fashioned, but I try not to tackle the dishes in my sink without gloves. Excessive hand-washing—or prolonged exposure to water—can be hard on your manicure and may lead to dry and brittle nails.

INGREDIENTS TO AVOID

There are a lot of potentially harmful chemicals in nail polish and nail-polish remover. But that doesn't mean you can't get manicures! Below are a few ingredients to avoid when buying nail polish or when picking out a color at the salon; together, they have been referred to as the "toxic trio." A lot of great brands don't use these chemicals, so you should have no trouble finding the colors of your choice—just be sure to read the packaging carefully.

TOLUENE: Used to help nail polish go on smoothly, this is just bad news. It's a nervous-system toxin and can cause major irritation to the eyes and skin.

DIBUTYL PHTHALATE: Prevents nail polish from chipping. In studies with lab animals, it's been connected to cancer and can cause birth defects.

FORMALDEHYDE: Like with cosmetics (see page 25), formaldehyde is an all-too-common ingredient in nail products—in particular, nail hardener. It's a known carcinogen.

PRODUCTS AND TOOLS

Stocking up on products and tools for your nails is pretty straightforward and relatively inexpensive. You can buy a full set of tools at most pharmacies or beauty-supply stores and then replenish your products as needed.

NAIL CLIPPER: Used to trim your nails. These come in different shapes and sizes.

NAIL FILE: Used to shape and smooth the tips of your nails. Choose a metal nail file that you can clean with soap and water. A high-number file, which means the grain is finer, will help you achieve a smoother edge.

BUFFER: Buffing the surface of your nails creates a glossy look. This is a great alternative to polish.

CUTICLE PUSHER: You want to push down your cuticles for better nail health. It can also make your nails look cleaner and prettier because more of the nail will be exposed. Pick a cuticle pusher that you can clean with soap and water.

CUTICLE OIL: This will help moisturize your nail and the skin surrounding it, keeping them both conditioned and healthy. I like to apply this at least three times a week.

BASE COAT: This should be applied directly to clean nails before any other polish. Some of these contain nutrients that can help prevent the breakage, splitting, and peeling of your nails.

NAIL BRUSH: Clean under your nails with some gentle soap, warm water, and a nail brush.

TOP COAT: A clear top coat can extend the life of your manicure and helps add shine.

NAIL POLISH: A colored lacquer applied to the nails, aka the fun part. There is no shortage of options here but try to choose one free of the toxic trio.

NAIL-POLISH REMOVER: Applied with a cotton ball, this solvent is used to remove any nail polish or oils on the surface of the nail.

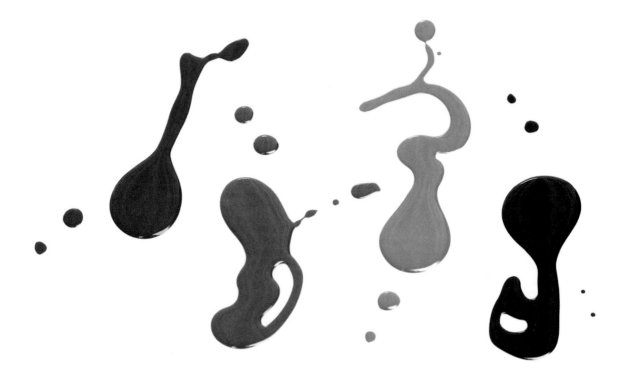

MANICURES

You have so many options when it comes to painting your nails, and it's easy to do at home, so why not skip the salon and do it yourself? This is definitely a skill you get better at with practice, so the more often you give yourself manicures, the better you'll get at them. Some basic and not-so-basic manicures to get you started are on the following pages.

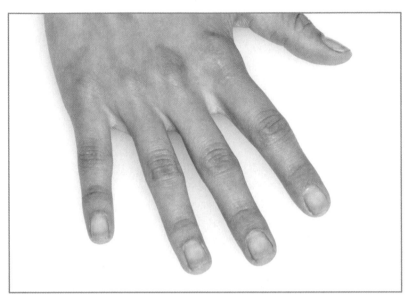

PRODUCTS AND TOOLS: Clippers, file, cuticle moisturizer and pusher, buffer.

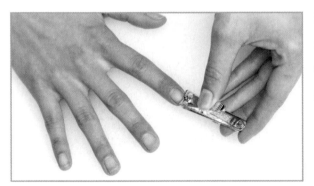

STEP 1: Begin with polish-free fingernails. Trim nails with nail clipper. I only trim my nails if they're super-long; otherwise I go straight to the nail file to get a more precise result.

STEP 2: Refine shape with nail file. Mastering the nail file will help you get a nice shape and is the best way for managing the length of your nails (and eliminating any pesky nail splinters left from trimming). People have strong nail-shape preferences—I like a natural-looking, squared-off oval. It's the easiest shape to get and the most elongating on my hand.

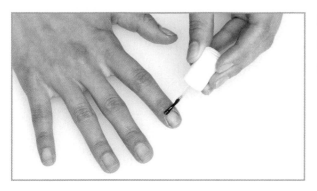

STEP 3: Moisturize your cuticles by rubbing cuticle oil into the nail and the perimeter where the nail meets your skin.

STEP 4: Push back cuticles. Unless you're a trained manicurist, in which case you are likely not reading my DIY manicure tips, *do not* trim your cuticles. There are conditioning removers for that. It's best to gently push the cuticles back after a shower when your skin is nice and soft. Apply the cuticle remover or cuticle oil. Be gentle! This is a delicate area.

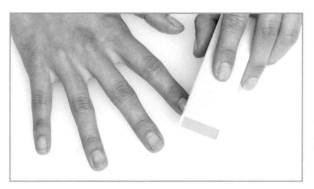

STEP 5: Buff! I love a buffed nail. It looks so clean, shiny, and healthy. This is a treat when I choose to go without colored polish, although I don't do this too frequently, because you're literally taking layers off your nails. Buff in Xes on the surface of your nail (so, diagonally across in each direction).

PRODUCTS AND TOOLS: File, polish remover, base coat, polish, top coat.

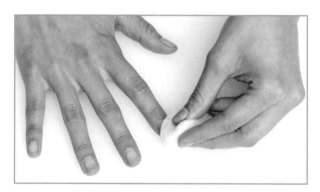

STEP 1: Refine shape with file as necessary, then clean nails with acetone-free nail-polish remover. Even if your nails are color-free, you need to remove the top layer of oil before you apply polish. It will help the color last longer.

STEP 2: Apply a base coat. This will protect your nails from getting stained through long-term nail-polish use. (Think of it as a barrier to any chemicals too, so choose one that is non-toxic.)

STEP 3: Apply color evenly on each nail. If necessary add a second coat.

STEP 4: Wait a few minutes for the color to dry, then add a clear top coat.

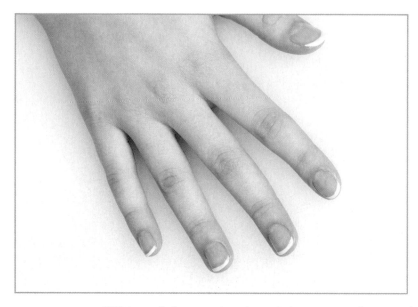

PRODUCTS AND TOOLS: White polish, paintbrush, polish remover, sheer pink polish, top coat.

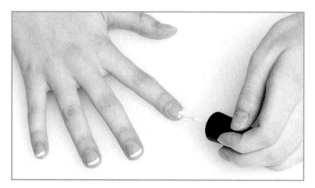

STEP 1: Paint the tips of your nails white. It doesn't have to be perfect, just evenly painted.

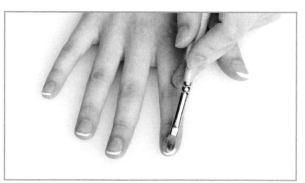

STEP 2: Using a brush with a rounded tip, dip in polish remover and clean up and smooth by dragging it along the inside of the white line (known as the smile line—it's where your nail bed ends). Wait a few minutes for the white to dry.

STEP 3: Apply one coat of sheer pink all over your nail.

STEP 4: Wait five minutes, then finish with a clear top coat.

REVERSE FRENCH MANICURE

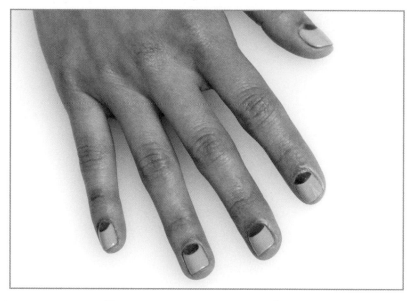

PRODUCTS AND TOOLS: Base coat, two contrasting colors, top coat.

STEP 1: Apply a base coat.

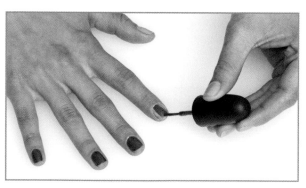

STEP 2: Apply the bottom coat on the whole nail. We started with a shimmery blue. Wait five minutes for the coat to dry.

STEP 3: Paint the next coat in a contrasting color, leaving a half-circle, mimicking the shape of the little moon at the base of your nail.

TIP: You can use adhesive hole reinforcements to help get the right shape. Just make sure the base color has dried completely before you stick anything to your nails.

STEP 4: Wait five minutes, then finish with a clear top coat.

POLKA DOTS WITH THREE COLORS

PRODUCTS AND TOOLS: Base coat, one light color, three bright colors, small paintbrush, top coat.

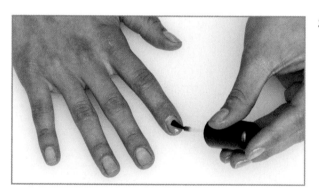

STEP 1: Apply base coat.

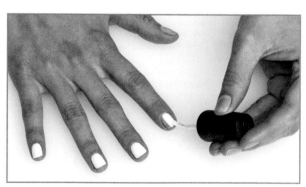

STEP 2: Paint each nail white or an opaque light color that the others will pop on.

STEP 3: Paint three dots on each nail, one in each color (roughly in a triangle form).

STEP 4: Complete each color before moving on to the next.

STEP 5: Wait five to ten minutes, then finish with a clear top coat.

FLOWERS

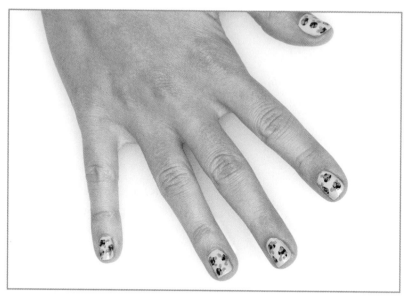

PRODUCTS AND TOOLS: Base coat, base color, two colors for flower, green polish, paintbrush, polish remover, top coat.

STEP 1: Apply a base coat.

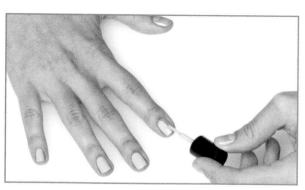

STEP 2: Paint your nails a solid color. It should be light enough to serve as a good canvas. Wait ten minutes for it to dry.

STEP 3: Using a small paintbrush, paint the flower with a dark pink—you're going for a small, imperfect circle. You want two to four on each nail. Wait a few minutes for the polish to dry.

STEP 4: Using the small paintbrush (clean it with polish remover first), dot the center of each flower once or twice with a lighter pink. Wait a few minutes for the polish to dry.

STEP 5: With a dark green polish, make the leaves by painting small dots next to each flower (one or two dots per flower).

STEP 6: Wait five minutes, then finish with a clear top coat.

245

GLITTER

PRODUCTS AND TOOLS: Base coat, fine-grain glitter, top coat.

STEP 1: Apply a base coat to one hand.

STEP 2: Before that coat has a chance to dry, dip each finger in a fine glitter (which you can get at any art-supplies store). Repeat on the other hand.

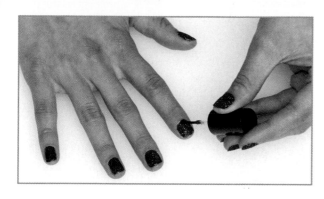

STEP 3: Apply two top-coat layers. (The second layer is to give you a smoother surface.)

TIP: You can use clear tape to remove stray glitter around your cuticles.

CHAPTER TWELVE
Beauty Through the Decades

*D*o you ever feel like you were born in the wrong decade? My great-grandma Truly was a cigarette girl back in the 1920s, and often I find myself dreaming of what life may have been like back then. I imagine ringing my eyes in black shadow, painting on my cupid's bow with a vamp lipstick, and spending my evenings draped in hand-beading while frequenting speakeasies (because nothing would come between me and a glass of champagne . . . not even Prohibition). And other times I like to picture myself with softly applied makeup and a flawless '50s updo, wearing pearls and an apron as I pop dinner into the oven and I complete my daily chores. These were years when women really took the time to put themselves together; whether it was to spend an evening listening to jazz or simply to serve their family a hot meal, they did it with style. And while we have come so far in so many areas, I can't help but notice that we've lost a bit of our glamour along the way. This is one of the many reasons why I love to incorporate trends from the past into my looks. I like making the extra effort even if it's not necessary by today's standards.

The past century was filled with trailblazing women who, instead of following the trends, set their own. For each decade a handful of women evoke the times, and beginning in the '20s, which was definitely the start of a "beauty culture," it was often Hollywood's magic that created these icons: The dark-haired, bob-cut-adorned Louise Brooks represented the beauty ideal in the '20s; the quintessential blond bombshell Marilyn Monroe with her bright blue eyes accented with cat-eye liner and her platinum hair was an icon of the '50s; Twiggy's pixie cut and mod eye set the tone for the '60s; the all-American, feather-haired and bronzed skin Farrah Fawcett was the look of the '70s; and so on. . . . These were the women who would set the style for years to come.

Everything in this book (and in your store of beauty products) can be traced to a beauty invention or trend from history. Here's a quick look back at some of the highlights from decades past that I found most interesting:

1920s

During the Jazz Age, Coco Chanel referred to a suntan as a "fashion accessory," and women began wearing orange-hued makeup to give the illusion of a tan. Long hair and all its attendant needs was no longer coveted as women freed themselves from their locks in favor of the Eton crop. Lipstick cost a dime a tube, and no respectable flapper would go partying without hers. Max Factor became the first makeup artist to the stars.

1930s

The dawn of the platinum blonde! This was also a time for Hollywood starlets to stealthily undergo nips and tucks—actresses like Marlene Dietrich achieved DIY face-lift results with tape and clips around her hairline. Plus motion pictures were in color now, so moviegoers could actually see (and covet) the effects of cosmetics. Makeup and skin care became a necessity for all, and the birth of companies like Revlon helped get products to the masses. (Revlon's first claim to fame was revolutionizing nail polish so it stayed on the nails.) Oh, and this was also the decade that ushered in painted toenails— because open-toed shoes became popular.

1940s

Long hair was so in fashion that *Life* magazine ran a story about Veronica Lake's 'do. Toward the beginning of war rationing, makeup was the first to go, but demand for it won out in the end, even if the pickings were slim. Since stockings weren't available during the war, women turned to leg makeup (really!), even painting a line up the back of their legs to give the illusion of a seam. Once the war ended, the floodgates opened, and women could again have their red lipstick and the newly commercially available fake eyelashes and liquid eyeliner.

1950s

The '50s housewife is an icon of her own, and this was the first decade where teen girls started to have an influence in the marketplace. TV gave everyone more varieties of role models, and cosmetics, as an industry, continued to flourish. Working woman or housewife . . . nobody left home without her lipstick on.

1960s

During this time a pale complexion became popular and skirts got really short—this was the decade the miniskirt was invented. (Even the leg makeup came back. . . .) For makeup, the eyes were a focus: lots of mascara and then false eyelashes (which apparently lasted a week!). Cover Girl debuted and was one of the first cosmetics aimed at teens.

1970s

Bell-bottoms and platform shoes (which would come back eventually . . .) were the calling card of this decade, which wasn't subtle in the least (hello, disco). The quality of makeup improved with creamier formulas and smoother textures, and even the tools of the trade got a face-lift, with higher-quality brushes now available. The big beauty innovation was definitely lip gloss, which really became a must-have product.

1980s

Shoulder pads and big hair met strong colors and an ever-growing cosmetics industry, and by the '80s there was a product for pretty much anything . . . much like there is today. Workout videos and low-fat foods become a regular thing, no doubt fueled by the fact that models were becoming "supermodels" and everyone knew their names and faces.

1990s & BEYOND

In the '90s, style became more casual and makeup went neutral and natural again. This was the decade of grunge after all and appearing polished wasn't exactly a goal of that movement—looking disheveled was all part of the aesthetic. But this was also the decade of the movie *Clueless* and Jennifer Aniston's famous hairstyle from *Friends* (aka The Rachel), so clearly some people were paying attention to more than flannel shirts and messy hair. Tattoos and piercings hit the mainstream, and nail-polish color options expanded and got sparkly (and came from companies with names like Hard Candy and Urban Decay). And after years of being sought after to work on Hollywood celebrities and models, makeup artists like Bobbi Brown and Kevyn Aucoin, who both championed a natural look, were becoming celebrities themselves in the cosmetics industry, both eventually launching their own lines.

Trends from the past are constantly reappearing in the present. Fashion designers, makeup artists, and hairstylists often look back for inspiration and find new ways to reinterpret and update different periods so that they feel modern and fresh. That's why I wanted to look back, too.

This chapter is all about celebrating the iconic women of the past century who established new paradigms of beauty. And in the process, it's also about figuring out what you find relatable and making it work for you. My amazing beauty team and I re-created some looks wholesale from different decades—just to hammer it home (and honestly, we couldn't help ourselves)—but there's no reason you can't appropriate just one element. You can find a hairstyle or a makeup trick from another era and make it your own. (We stopped after the '70s, because of course I'm most interested in the decades I didn't live through.) And keep in mind that there are many beauties beyond the ones whose looks we're replicating here—I chose to channel the women whose features most closely resemble my own, and as you look for inspiration, you should do the same!

THE '20S: THE WILD FLAPPERS

In the early 1900s, women generally had long, pinned-up hair and wore constricting corsets and gowns, but that all changed with the Roaring '20s. Women won the right to vote, joined the workforce, and were finally allowed to compete in the Olympic Games. Hemlines got much shorter, and silhouettes got a lot less body-conscious (so women could dance, swim, and play sports)—and haircuts got shorter too. The decade ushered in painted nails and the bob, which was pretty scandalous at first, though quickly embraced by women everywhere because it was liberating, fun, and an appropriate illustration of the sexual revolution of the times. The women who represented the times include Louise Brooks, Clara Bow, Mary Pickford, Josephine Baker, and Gloria Swanson.

Unless you have a bob cut, there's no way to approximate the look without resorting to a wig. If you have a bob cut, you can use a flatiron to make it sleek and then a curling iron to get the shape to arc away from your face, and then you'll be looking flapper chic.

Eye makeup was heavy, and brows were extremely thin, so if you want to channel the '20s, you'll need black eyeliner and eye shadow. (And you should line both your upper and lower lash line.) A cupid's bow lip was popular, so pick a dark, vampy color. Use lip liner to create the bow by making a little dot at the two highest points of the upper lip, at the bottom of the bow, and in the corners. Then connect the dots with a line that swoops a bit down. The '20s lip is small, so it may actually be within your real line. Our lips aren't generally symmetrical, so you may need to refine the shape with a pointed cotton swab, to create the illusion of a perfect bow.

THE '30S: THE COOL AND GLAMOROUS

After the roar of the '20s, life got more serious in the '30s. The Great Depression saw Americans out of work. (Many women were forbidden to take jobs that might otherwise go to men.) Many turned to the glamour and fairy-tale endings of movies for escape and comfort—women like Marlene Dietrich, Greta Garbo, Carole Lombard, and Jean Harlow were the beauty ideal. But it was also a time of important strides in the feminist movement: Jane Addams became the first American woman to win a Nobel Peace Prize (she worked with the poor), Amelia Earhart took flight, and First Lady Eleanor Roosevelt held her own press conferences (and allowed only female reporters to attend). Women looked polished and intense but feminine too.

Hair was structured and textured, so getting the look involves a lot of curling and teasing. If you have long hair like I do, you can hide your length. The secret is two braids in the back, pinned flat against your head with large bobby pins.

This look is all about the brows. To achieve it you have to "erase" yours first so you can draw a thin line above them. Obviously that's not something you'd want to incorporate into your everyday routine. If you want to try it for a costume, you'll need spirit gum, spirit-gum remover (don't forget this!), eyebrow wax, and a metal spatula, plus a lot of cream foundation. Then with a black or dark brown pencil, sharpened to a thin point, you can draw in elongated, pencil-thin brows that are rounded at the corners. A strong lip completes the look—try a bright red lip liner and lipstick. Finish with some clear gloss.

THE '40S: THE STRONG AND SERIOUS

Golf, baseball, and wartime jobs in steel plants launched the famous "We Can Do It!" campaign . . . and women did do it. Men were at war, so women embraced the business of making it all happen at home. Like in the '30s, beauty in this period was serious and understated, but with more emphasis on looking natural (no more painted-on, pencil-thin brows). In part, this is because of extreme shortages, but also because it was a time for expressing a more practical approach to beauty. Fashion was functional until the end of the war ushered in the New Look—and Christian Dior—with its full skirts and petticoats and hats. Long-haired beauties like Veronica Lake, Ava Gardner, Rita Hayworth, Lauren Bacall, and Lena Horne (the first black actor to get a major contract with a Hollywood studio) were approachable yet mysterious.

This is a look you can definitely take inspiration from for a glamorous night out. Women's hairstyles softened from the previous decades and tended to be worn longer and with soft waves. Back then they used cake liner on their eyes, which can still be found today at beauty-supply stores, but you can replicate it easily by wetting a thin liner brush and dipping it into a black shadow, or you can use black kohl liner or liquid liner. Sweep it along the upper lash line, then flick it at the end. Mascara was used to darken lashes more intensely on the outer edge of the eyes. Complete the look with bright red lip liner and a pretty red lipstick. Skip the gloss, since you want the look to be matte.

THE '50S: THE CLASSIC BEAUTIES AND BLOND BOMBSHELLS

Despite major strides in the civil rights movement—Rosa Parks refused to give up her seat on a bus, while Althea Gibson, the first African American to play in the U.S. Open, won two titles—this was a period of feminist backlash. Since men were back from the war, women were expected to return to the role of housewife. Some of the most hyperfeminine—and hypersexed—icons emerged: This was Marilyn Monroe's heyday, after all! Pinup beauty went mainstream in a big way. But this was also the decade of Grace Kelly, Elizabeth Taylor, and Audrey Hepburn, each woman showcasing different beauty ideals, each one admired by men and women alike.

The look was feminine and feel-good. Even the preferred body type shifted as women aspired to a curvy hourglass figure. The color palette for makeup consisted of soft pastels for the lips and cheeks, and bright hues for the eyes. Brows remained strong and the lashes were full. Strip lashes provided a doll-like quality to eyes. Hair was meticulously styled, often set in updos and finished with accessories.

THE '60S: THE REPRESSED AND THE REVOLUTIONARY

A sexual revolution was brewing (Woodstock capped off this decade), but in the beginning of the '60s, beauty became a little more uptight: Both hair and makeup were a bit sculpted and exaggerated, really as a way to draw attention to the artifice of beauty. Near the end of the decade, this began to change: The miniskirt made its appearance, along with a more global appreciation of beauty, with stars like Sophia Loren making a splash alongside Brigitte Bardot, Julie Christie, and Faye Dunaway, and international models like Twiggy and Veruschka.

Hair had volume in the sixties, so go get yourself some hot rollers and a good comb for teasing. Another popular style in this decade was the close-cropped pixie look.

Skin was pale and brows were strong. You can get the brows by using an eyebrow powder or pencil that's one shade darker than your natural color. The shape should be more severe, so avoid rounding the edges. Lashes and liner were strong, too. To get a spidery, more defined effect on your lashes, use the tip of the mascara brush where there's more product to coat both your top and bottom lashes. Or, you can use a strip lash. Line your water line with a nude or white-colored pencil to open up the eye. Balance the eyes (which often were done in frosted colors) with a soft peachy-pink lipstick.

THE '70S: THE FREE SPIRITS

The hippies of the late '60s ushered in a whole new style of beauties: the long-haired, tawny-skinned ladies of the '70s who worked their bell-bottoms, maxi skirts, and all manner of platform shoe. From the bouncy, feathered hairdos to the natural-looking makeup (it was the first time makeup was marketed as "invisible"), the look was breezy and free, exemplified by women like Farrah Fawcett, Jane Fonda, Lauren Hutton, Iman, Ali MacGraw, and Goldie Hawn. It was the beginning of one of my favorite beauty trends: effortless glamour.

Hair was parted down the middle and curled/feathered out and away from the face using hot rollers and lots of hair spray (or women willing to commit to curls went for a perm). Like the hair, the makeup was light and breezy. Since sun-kissed skin was popular, bronzer and terra-cotta-colored blush were a must, as was a little touch of shimmer. Eyes were washed with matte earth-toned shadows (or pastels and metallics if you were in the mood to disco). Brows went natural and lashes were also feathery and natural-looking. Lips could be finished with a glossy, skin-toned lip color for a healthy, low-key look.

ACKNOWLEDGMENTS

A lot of people were involved in the making of this book, but special thanks go to:

Angela Kohler and Ithyle Griffiths for doing such a lovely job with the photography, and Shiloh Strong, Ian Grieve, and Mallory Morrison for helping every step of the way.

Kristin Ess and Caityln Rylander for creating so many amazing hairstyles. No one does it quite like you ladies.

Amy Nadine Rosenberg, Phoebe Dawson, and Sophia Flores for leaving no lash out of place and no nose un-powdered. Your attention to detail was more than appreciated.

Ashlie Johnson for providing such pretty manicures and being a joy to work with.

Tara Swennen and Sydney Lopez for taking so much time to style each look. I loved playing dress-up with you girls!

Farrin Jacobs for working harder than any editor should ever have to, to get a book done by its deadline. Between traveling across the country and working countless late nights you really went above and beyond. This book literally would not be possible without all your hard work and dedication. So thank you!!

Elise Loehnen for being such an amazing partner. I am so thrilled we were able to create yet another book together.

Juliana Friedman for sharing your skin-care expertise with us.

Siren Studios for being so accommodating to our crew. And our beautiful models for being patient and pleasant.

The authors of two books that were helpful in researching the Beauty through the Decades chapter (and confirming what we thought we already knew!): *Decades of Beauty* by Kate Mulvey and Melissa Richards (Checkmark Books, 1998) and *Classic Beauty: The History of Makeup* by Gabriela Hernandez (Schiffer Publishing, 2011).

The team at HarperCollins: Tom Forget (who also traveled across the country), Melinda Weigel, Gwen Morton, Josh Weiss, Barb Fitzsimmons, Christina Colangelo, Sandee Roston, Catherine Wallace, Randy Rosema, Sarah Landis, and Lillian Sun.

As always, thank you to the amazing people who work so hard every day to allow me to do the things I love. I am so lucky to be surrounded by such kind and talented people. So thank you to Max Stubblefield, Nicole Perez-Kruger, Kristin Puttkamer, Matthew Elblonk, PJ Shapiro, and Dave Del Sesto.

And of course an extra-special additional thank-you to my dear friends Amy Nadine Rosenberg and Kristin Ess for all of your valuable input while writing many of the chapters in this book. I have loved the years we have spent working together. You have taught me about so much more than just hair and makeup.

Credits

PHOTOGRAPHY
Angela Kohler and Ithyle Griffiths

MAKEUP
Amy Nadine Rosenberg

HAIR
Kristin Ess

NAILS
Ashlie Johnson

FASHION
Tara Swennen and Sydney Lopez

Fashion Credits

COVER AND INTRODUCTION: Dress by Manuela.

CHAPTER 1: Dress by Alberto Makali; necklace by Elisa Solomon.

CHAPTER 3: Shirt by Joie.

CHAPTER 4: Shirt by Covet; tank top by Champion; workout pants by Nux; necklace by Charlotte Lu.

CHAPTER 5: Tank top by Fila; workout pants by Nux. Page 71, sneakers by Asics.

CHAPTER 6: Dress by Maria Lucia Hohan; bracelets by Melinda Maria.

CHAPTER 7: Shirt by Helmut Lang; necklace by Dana Rebecca.

CHAPTER 8: Dress by Jenny Packham. Shirt worn with everyday waves by Vanessa Bruno.

CHAPTER 9: Shirt by Rebecca Taylor. Shirt worn with all braids by Ecoté.

CHAPTER 10: Dress by Lorena Sarbu. Shirt worn with loose ponytail by BCBGeneration. Shirts worn with retro curl and curling with a wand by Sabine.

CHAPTER 11: Shirt by Market; jeans by 7 For All Mankind; rings by Alexandra Jefford and Le Vian.

CHAPTER 12: Vintage dress from Janey Lopaty; gloves and feather hairpiece are vintage.

'20s: Dress by Gryphon; shoes by Jimmy Choo; vintage pearls from Janey Lopaty.

'30s: Dress by Stella & Jamie; necklace by Banana Republic; vintage bracelets from Janey Lopaty.

'40s: Dress by Michael Kors; brooch worn as barrette is vintage.

'50s: Vintage dress from Janey Lopaty; gloves and feather hairpiece are vintage.

'60s: Vintage dress from Janey Lopaty.

'70s: Dress by Issa; shoes by H&M.

Photo Credits

All photos © Angela + Ithyle except the following:

page 12 All images courtesy of Lauren Conrad except lower right image © Stephen Shugerman/Getty Images, Inc.

page 13 (clockwise from top left) © Jeffrey Mayer/Getty Images, Inc.; © Steve Granitz/Getty Images, Inc.; © Ethan Miller/Getty Images, Inc.; © Donato Sardella/Getty Images, Inc.

page 18 © istockphoto.com/Plainview

page 21 © Jonathan Kantor/Getty Images, Inc.

page 23 © Studio 504/Getty Images, Inc.

page 26 © Shutterstock/LVV

page 30 © Shutterstock/kuleczka

page 38 © Shutterstock/Picsfive

page 41 © Shutterstock/Valentyn Volkov

page 49 © Shutterstock/shutswis

page 50 © Shutterstock/Rob Bouwman

page 60 © Shutterstock/Jetrel

page 104 © Shutterstock/ocram

page 107 Fan brush © Shutterstock/oksana2010

page 176 © istockphoto.com/mosutatsu

page 229 © istockphoto.com/Green_Leaf

page 232 © Shutterstock/travis manley

page 257 Mary Pickford © Michael Ochs Archives/Getty Images, Inc.; Louise Brooks,